# THE TESTIMONY OF
# POETS
# AND SAGES

## THE PSALMS AND
## WISDOM LITERATURE

W. H. Bellinger, Jr.

SMYTH&HELWYS
PUBLISHING, INCORPORATED    MACON, GEORGIA

ISBN 1-57312-004-9

*The Testimony of Poets and Sages*
*The Psalms and Wisdom Literature*

W. H. Bellinger, Jr.

Copyright © 1998

Smyth & Helwys Publishing, Inc.
6316 Peake Road
Macon, Georgia 31210-3960
1-800-747-3016

*Library of Congress Cataloging-in-Publication Data*

Bellinger, W. H.
    The testimony of poets and sages: the psalms and wisdom
literature / W. H. Bellinger.
    p. cm. — (All the Bible)
    ISBN 1-57312-004-9      (alk. paper)
    1. Bible.  O.T.  Psalms—Criticism, interpretation, etc.
    2. Wisdom Literature—Criticism, interpretation, etc.
    I. Title.
    II. Series.
BS1410.B45        1998
223'.061—dc21                                          98-16750
                                                           CIP

# Contents

Preface
**Reading as a Journey**                                    v

Chapter 1
**Psalms: Prayer Book of the Bible**                        1

Chapter 2
**Reading the Psalms**                                      9

Chapter 3
**Prayer and Praise in the Psalms**                        33

Chapter 4
**What Is Wisdom?**                                         51

Chapter 5
**Proverbs: Wisdom for Full Living**                       61

Chapter 6
**Job: Wisdom in Dialogue**                                75

Chapter 7
**Ecclesiastes: Search for Meaning**                       95

Conclusion
**The Testimony of Poets and Sages**                      103

Preface

# Reading as a Journey

We take many journeys in life—to visit friends, to vacation, to buy groceries, to see special sites, to go to work. Some of our journeys do not include geographical movement, however. We may take an imaginary trip to a special place or setting. We also use "journey" as a metaphor for life or for the pilgrimage of faith. We move through the various experiences that comprise our lives.

In this volume I propose that we extend that metaphor to the experience of reading. Readers often travel with an author through the plot of a story; we can do the same with the Old Testament books of poetry and wisdom. We can follow the road set out in these books, and eventually that road can become part of our path for life.

So I invite you to join me on a trip. Bring your imagination, your mind, your spirit—your whole self—and journey with me through the delightful and insightful worlds of the books of Psalms, Proverbs, Job, and Ecclesiastes. The testimony of Old Testament poets and sages can become part of our path for living, enriching the pilgrimage of faith.

A significant part of my vocational calling is the communication of the fruits of biblical scholarship to the church. Thus, I appreciate the opportunity to participate in a series such as *All the Bible*. I am grateful for the invitation from Dr. Page Kelley, the general editor of the Old Testament volumes until the time of his death in 1997. Kelley's life of scholarship, teaching, and ministry made a lasting contribution to Baptists. Likewise, I am grateful to the folks at Smyth & Helwys for their expertise and commitment. Others who helped with this manuscript include Robert Baker, Carolyn Edwards, Clova Gibson, and John Vassar. My wife, Libby, continues to be my best editor. I also express appreciation to my colleagues at Baylor University for a context in which to conduct research and to many other scholars whose work I have consulted.

# Chapter 1

# Psalms

# Prayer Book of the Bible

The book of Psalms is the most read and used of all the books in the Old Testament. The Psalms have influenced many persons of faith and communities of faith. I have known many people who have turned to this book in times of trouble and who read these texts regularly. Certainly one of the reasons for the popularity of the book is that it relates to every conceivable human experience, from joy to sorrow, from anger to reconciliation, and all sorts of conditions in between. These conditions of life move the speakers in the Psalms to pray. And so readers today can learn much of the life of prayer and faith in these texts. Accordingly, the book has been called "The Prayer Book of the Bible." Any journey of reading will have beginning points. In the case of the Psalms, one of those beginning points is that much of this book is addressed to God as prayer. Another is the shape of the book as it appears in our Old Testament. The organization of any text provides a context for reading.

## Background

### Title

The first matter to consider when observing the organization of the book of Psalms is the title. Three titles for the book are noteworthy. The first is the one I have been using so far, the Psalms. This word is a transliteration of the title of the book from the Greek translation or version of the Old Testament called the Septuagint. That explains the odd English spelling of the name; it simply brings the word from Greek into English letters. The

Greek title refers to songs accompanied by stringed instruments. A second title readers may recognize comes from the Latin version of the Old Testament called the Vulgate. The Latin word is brought into English to make another unusual word, Psalter. This term refers to the stringed instrument accompanying the songs. The other significant title is the one that would have been used earlier than either the Greek or Latin titles, that is, the title of the Hebrew book—*Sepher Tehillim*. The Hebrew title, meaning "Book of Praises," may be the most appropriate for the book. So the titles give us a first clue as to the nature of these texts; they are songs or praises performed with musical accompaniment.

## Structure

The second matter to consider about the organization of the book of Psalms is the structure. The book is not composed of chapters but of 150 songs or psalms organized into five divisions or books. Just as there are five books of law in the books of Moses that begin the Old Testament, so there are five books of psalms in response.

|          |                 |
|----------|-----------------|
| Book I   | Psalms 1–41     |
| Book II  | Psalms 42–72    |
| Book III | Psalms 73–89    |
| Book IV  | Psalms 90–106   |
| Book V   | Psalms 107–150  |

Each book concludes with a benediction, a word of blessing and thanksgiving to God, especially for the psalms in the book that is concluding (Pss 41:13; 72:18-20; 89:52; 106:48). These benedictions technically belong to the whole book and not just the psalm immediately preceding. The texts are similar; Psalm 72:18-20 provides the fullest example:

> Blessed be the Lord, the God of Israel,
>     who alone does wondrous things.
> Blessed be his glorious name forever;
>     may his glory fill the whole earth.
>     Amen and Amen.
> The prayers of David son of Jesse are ended.

Psalm 150 serves as a powerful benediction for both the fifth book and for the entire Psalter.

As Psalm 150 serves as a conclusion to the Psalter, so Psalm 1 provides an introduction. This introductory psalm sets out two ways of life, the righteous and the wicked, and calls upon readers to choose between the two. The righteous or wise, reflecting the preferable lifestyle, will avoid evil and meditate on God's instruction. This psalm suggests that the Psalter becomes part of God's instruction or *torah*—God's teaching, guidance, will, revelation for living the life of faith and especially for that dimension so central to the life of faith, prayer. Psalm 2 articulates the same lifestyle question for nations and so is also part of the introduction. Its question is whether nations will serve God and God's anointed or rebel against the one authority who can give fullness of life, God. The 150 psalms, then, move from this emphasis on obedience to the unbridled praise of God in the concluding Psalm 150, a sign that the righteous life is rewarding.

## Superscriptions

Another dimension of the organization of the Psalter is the superscriptions. Most of the psalms have a superscription or brief title written above the text. In the Hebrew Bible, the superscription is the first verse of the psalm. These superscriptions are not all the same, but they often contain three elements.

- *Liturgical Collections*—Phrases such as "A Psalm of the Korahites" or "A Psalm of Asaph" indicate the collection from which the psalm came.

- *Technical Terms Related to Worship*—Phrases such as "To the leader: according to Lilies" apparently relate to the use of the psalm in worship.

- *Historical Notes*—Some superscriptions associate their psalm with events in the life of David and so provide an actual life setting in which to read the prayer. Psalm 59 illustrates: "when Saul ordered his house to be watched in order to kill him" (David).

Psalm 57 provides a good example of a full superscription: "To the leader: Do Not Destroy [technical terms related to worship]. Of David [liturgical collection]. A Miktam, when he fled from Saul, in the cave [historical note]."

## Collections

Attention to the superscriptions leads to one additional subject in the organization of the book of Psalms, the collections contained in the book. A number of superscriptions refer to collections. The first half of the Psalter is dominated by Davidic psalms, but there are also Korahite and Asaphite psalms and other collections. The book is a collection of collections.

| | |
|---|---|
| Davidic Collections | 3–41; 51–72; 138–145 |
| Korahite Collections | 42–49; 84–85; 87–88 |
| Elohistic Psalter | 42–83 |
| Asaphite Collections | 73–83 |
| Psalms on the Kingship of God | 93–100 |
| A Collection of Psalms of Praise | 103–107 |
| Songs of Ascents | 120–134 |
| Hallelujah Psalms | 111–118; 146–150 |

These collections have been brought together to make up our book of Psalms and have been shaped in a purposeful way. It would be appropriate to comment on two collections.

The Elohistic Psalter, Psalms 42–83, gets its name from its penchant to use "Elohim"—God—rather than "Yahweh"—the Lord—when referring to the deity. Compilers of this group of psalms for some reason have preferred the more generic "Elohim" for God. The other collection that deserves comment is the Davidic psalms. The tradition relating David to psalmody is clear and significant in the Old Testament, but that judgment is based on more than the evidence in the superscriptions of the Psalms. A number of psalms are titled "of David." The Hebrew term used contains the name David *david* and the preposition *le*. This preposition can mean a variety of things such as "to, for, belonging to, with reference to, on behalf of." Some scholars have suggested the term indicates Davidic authorship, but the significance of the Hebrew word is far from clear. I suspect the phrase means belonging to David or to the Davidic line of kings in the sense that this psalm comes from a Davidic hymnbook, a Davidic collection of psalms. This collection carried the official royal, Davidic stamp of approval for use in worship in Jerusalem. David was the one who gave the initial impetus and support for using psalms in worship in Jerusalem. Clearly David was the patron of psalmody in ancient Israel. He no doubt gave much impetus to the writing of psalms and to their use in worship in Jerusalem. I fully expect that he wrote psalms, but the superscriptions in the Psalter provide little evidence on the matter.

The title, structure, superscriptions, and collections of the Psalter provide some initial clues for reading these songs that have been purposefully collected into our Old Testament book.

## The Psalms as Poetry

The book of Psalms is in large measure a book of poetic prayers, and readers need to attend to the poetic dimension of these songs. Hebrew poetry is somewhat different than traditional English poetry, which focuses on sound rhyme, as seen in the example:

Jack and Jill
went up the hill

Hebrew poetry apparently had a kind of meter to it, but the pattern of that meter has been lost in the mists of time. We do know that Hebrew poetry had a kind of thought rhythm, which is central to the form. Central to this rhythm is what we call *parallelism*. Hebrew poems move on parallel words and lines and larger sections. English translations of these poems can capture this memorable parallel structure, especially with parallel lines. One line of a Hebrew verse makes a statement, and the second is in some sense parallel to the first; the second line echoes or seconds the first in some way. Three main types of parallel lines have been suggested.

- *Synonymous*—The second line echoes the first with a similar thought, like a synonym. The second line is not identical but similar.

> Why do the nations conspire,
>> and the peoples plot in vain? (2:1)

- *Antithetic*—The second line presents a contrast to the first line, the other side of the coin, and so the two lines together complete a thought. The second line is the antithesis or opposite of the first.

> For the arms of the wicked shall be broken,
>> but the Lord upholds the righteous. (37:17)

- *Stair-step*—The second line takes another step in the thought of the verse. This third type of parallelism is sometimes called synthetic or formal parallelism.

> O give thanks to the Lord, for he is good;
>> for his steadfast love endures forever. (107:1)

Parallel lines produce a striking echo effect that readers will do well to notice in the Psalms. But we should not think of the parallel lines as saying the same thing or think that there are only three kinds of parallel line structures. The relationship between lines in Hebrew poetry is multifaceted. Still, the examples above illustrate the kind of thought rhyme and parallel structure characteristic of Hebrew poetry. Attention to these and other poetic devices will help the interpreter. We will return to these issues in the next chapter. This brief description of Hebrew poetry applies to Proverbs, Job, and Ecclesiastes as well as the Psalms.

The poetic dimension of the Psalms holds more than stylistic devices. It is helpful for readers to see that the Psalms are different in form from historical accounts or prose narratives, and so we read the Psalms differently. I have already described the Psalms as poetic prayers; they are in a sense a response to God. Perhaps the best way of thinking about what the Psalms are is to describe them as *pilgrimage songs of faith*. They are the songs ancient Israel sang on pilgrimage to worship God at the

Temple. But there is also a broader sense in which life is a journey or pilgrimage. These are the songs the community sang while moving through the life of faith, the songs that kept them going. The songs articulated their faith and thus spoke to their faith. Anytime a person can articulate the experience of faith, he or she can give shape and definition to the experience and express it. Bernhard Anderson's introduction to the Psalms is entitled *Out of the Depths: The Psalms Speak for Us Today.* The Psalms derive from the depths of human experience and so can speak to us, but these songs also speak for us. They mouth our experience of faith even when we cannot.

So the Psalms are the community's public expressions of faith. As such, these texts also are central biblical examples of theology at its best. In the context of a worshiping community, the speakers in the Psalms seek to integrate reality, their own life experience, with the faith they have inherited. Sometimes reality squares with the faith, and praise comes forth. Sometimes reality challenges that faith, and questioning comes forth. And there are all shades in between. In this way these inspired poets of old sought to understand life from the faith dimension. The Psalms are a hymnbook or prayer book that articulates the faith of the believing community. The Psalms are thus central to the Old Testament, confessing its basic faith.

No wonder the Psalms have remained so popular and influential through the centuries. They touch the basic human experience and relate it to God's involvement in life. When readers see the Psalms as poetic prayers and so faith poems, new vistas of understanding can arise. The Psalms also relate to the broader context of the ancient Near East, which should be part of our introductory concerns. The nations surrounding ancient Israel also used psalms. Note two brief examples, first an Assyrian text (Anderson, p. 43).

> O Lord, decider of destinies of heaven and earth,
>     whose word no one alters,
> Who controls water and fire, leader of living creatures,
>     what god is like thee?
> In heaven who is exalted? Thou!
>     Thou alone art exalted.
> On earth who is exalted? Thou!
>     Thou alone art exalted.

Then notice a Babylonian prayer (Anderson, pp. 66-67).

How long. . . shall my adversaries be looking upon me,
In lying and untruth shall they plan evil against me,
Shall my pursuers and those who exult over me rage against me? . . .
Let my prayers and my supplications come to thee.
Let thy great mercy be upon me.

The poetry, language, and content of these psalms from other nations are similar to the psalms in the Old Testament. All of these texts show that psalmody was quite ancient in the Near East, and the Hebrew book of Psalms reflects that cultural background. Indeed, the whole of the Old Testament arose out of that sociohistorical context in the ancient Near East. Today's readers of these biblical texts will do well to note this perspective for it affirms that God was actually involved with those people in that time and that place. God did not simply appear to be involved, but was revealed in real life historical settings. And that leads to the primary way in which ancient Israel's psalmody is different from that of other nations. The Hebrew Psalms praise and pray to the one God of ancient Israel. The Psalms are a central expression of ancient Israel's distinctive faith. As pilgrimage songs of faith, they help enable the community to move forward in the life that faith makes possible.

## For Further Reading

Anderson, Bernhard W. *Out of the Depths: The Psalms Speak for Us Today.* Rev. ed. Philadelphia: Westminster Press, 1983.

Bellinger, W. H., Jr. *Psalms: Reading and Studying the Book of Praises.* Peabody MA: Hendrickson Publishers, 1990.

Bjornhard, Reidar B. "Psalms, Book of." In *Mercer Dictionary of the Bible,* ed. Watson Mills, 772-74. Macon GA: Mercer University Press, 1990.

Hopkins, Denise Dombkowski. "Poetry." In *Mercer Dictionary of the Bible,* ed. Watson Mills, 697-99. Macon GA: Mercer University Press, 1990.

Limburg, James. "Psalms, Book of." In *Anchor Bible Dictionary.* Vol. 5, 522-36. New York: Doubleday, 1992.

Chapter 2

# Reading the Psalms

I have invited us on a journey of reading the testimony of poets and sages, and we have begun that journey by looking at introductory issues in relation to the Psalms. The organization and poetry of the book have suggested some initial clues for reading. We have seen that the Psalms are prayer songs of the community expressing their faith and that these songs have been purposefully collected into our Old Testament book. Readers will gain from attending to the poetic dimensions of these texts. In addition to the context of the Old Testament book, readers will also want to learn from history how others have studied the Psalter. The history of scholarship is a real gift to us. From it we can learn of promises and pitfalls in the various ways of approaching our reading of the Psalms. Having looked initially at the form and shape of the book, we need to consider ways to approach it.

## A Form-Critical Approach

I have suggested that the Psalter can be viewed as both hymn book and prayer book. If we pursue the analogy with a hymn book and think about hymnals today, we realize that these collections tend to contain hymns of certain types, such as hymns of praise or hymns of dedication or commitment. The collections also contain hymns that are tied to certain worship settings, such as Easter hymns or Christmas carols. We can thus think about the hymns either in terms of content or use in worship. Psalm scholarship in the twentieth century has been dominated by an approach following that line of reasoning.

The man who pioneered this approach to the Psalms around the turn of the century was Hermann Gunkel. Gunkel sought a clear and logical method of study and took a clue from the field of botany. Botanists classify plants according to types, and Gunkel suggested that we can also classify the psalms according to type or kind or the form the psalm takes.

Gunkel's method centers on comparison. He considered the vocabulary of a psalm, the structure of a psalm, and the religious feeling exhibited in a psalm and began to arrange the psalms according to type. His study led him to the view that there are definable types of psalms with a fairly consistent form and content. He also came to the view that psalms of similar type came from a similar setting in the social and religious life of ancient Israel. With this method of classifying, Gunkel could list together all hymns of praise, all prayers for help, or all wisdom psalms. Then the interpreter could study all the hymns together and in comparison with the other kinds of psalms. One could also study a particular hymn of praise in light of the list of other hymns of praise. This approach provides a better basis for study, and it provided a new way forward for Psalms scholarship. Gunkel's form-critical or type-analytical approach is still the way most studies of the Psalms begin today. The term "form criticism" indicates a serious historical study of the forms or types of psalms.

Gunkel's study of the Psalms led him to describe five major types of psalms:

- *Hymns*—offer adoration and praise to the creator (ex.: Pss 8; 19). Gunkel distinguished three subtypes under this category: (1) Songs of Zion celebrate God's presence in Zion, or Jerusalem (ex.: Pss 46; 48). (2) Enthronement Psalms celebrate the kingship of God (ex.: Pss 47; 93). (3) Old Testament Hymns Outside the Psalter (ex.: Exod 15:1-18; 1 Sam 2:1-10).

- *Community Laments*—prayers for help in the midst of a crisis for the whole community such as military defeat or plague (ex.: Pss 44; 58).

- *Individual Laments*—prayers for help in the midst of crises such as sickness (ex.: Pss 3; 6). Gunkel listed one subtype under this category: Psalms of Trust express trust in the midst of the crisis at hand (ex.: Pss 11; 27).

- *Individual Psalms of Thanksgiving*—prayers of thanks when help arrives in a crisis (ex.: Pss 30; 32). These prayers come when the crisis has been resolved.

- *Royal Psalms*—come from various contexts in the life of the king in Jerusalem (ex.: Pss 2; 20). This category is not so much a category of form as are the other major types, and there are fewer Royal Psalms than the other major types. Still, Gunkel came to the view that the king was sufficiently important in ancient Israel's life that these texts be included as a major type.

Gunkel listed seven minor types of psalms:

- *Pilgrimage Songs*—Pilgrims sang these songs on the way to worship in the Temple (ex.: Pss 84; 122).

- *Community Psalms of Thanksgiving*—Just as individuals gave thanks for help, so did the community (ex.: Pss 67; 124).

- *Wisdom Psalms*—These texts provide wisdom for daily living, in line with the other wisdom books of Proverbs, Job, and Ecclesiastes (ex.: Pss 1; 49).

- *General Liturgies*—A liturgy is a text with a change of speaker, and general liturgies contain a variety of elements (ex.: Pss 60; 82).

- *Prophetic Liturgies*—These liturgies contain a prophetic warning (ex.: Pss 95; 126).

- *Entrance Liturgies*—These liturgies are instructions on who is qualified to enter the Temple for worship (ex.: Pss 15; 24).

- *Mixed Types*—These psalms contain elements of various types (ex.: Pss 9–10; 36).

This brief summary of Gunkel's categorization of the Psalms provides a helpful introduction to the content of the Psalter. The process of classification also provides a beneficial starting point for the study of the Psalms. It helps organize one's study of the Psalter and provides a good comparative base for beginning. Gunkel also began to ask the question of the setting from which these types of psalms arose. His answer centered on worship in ancient Israel. Others have pursued that matter. Gunkel's work brought a fresh start to Psalms study, and its impact has continued. Most classifications include the categories of hymn and lament as well as the distinction between individual and community psalms. The emphasis on the Royal Psalms has also continued.

Claus Westermann has offered a noteworthy refining of Gunkel's categories. He suggests two basic kinds of psalms: plea and praise, and the Psalms operate on a continuum between the cry for help or plea and praise. The movement is from plea to praise. Westermann has also seen that hymns and psalms of thanksgiving reflect two ways of performing the same activity: offering praise to God. A number of psalms cry for help in trouble. These pleas are on the way to thanksgiving when the help arrives. The thanksgiving psalm declares or narrates the story of how God has delivered from the crisis and in that way gives praise to God. The hymns describe God's activity in broader words of praise. Both types express praise to God.

The views of both Westermann and Gunkel are reflected in my classification chart of the Psalms. Many of the categories are Gunkel's. I have followed Westermann in placing the thanksgiving psalms under the category of praise. I have also suggested various kinds of hymns: Creation psalms, enthronement psalms, Zion psalms, trust psalms, and others. Such a classification is a helpful starting point in studying the Psalms. We will return to it frequently.

# A Classification of the Psalms

I. Hymns
A. General
29
33
68
100
103
105
111
113
114
115
117
134
135
139
145
146
147
149
150

B. On Creation
8
19
65
104
148

C. On Trust
23
91
121
125
131

D. Enthronement
Psalms
47
93
95
96
97
98
99

E. Zion Psalms
46
48
76
84
87
122

F. Entrance
Liturgies
15
24

G. Hymns with
Prophetic
Warnings
50
81
82

H. Individual
Thanksgivings
30
34
41
66
92
116

118
138

I. Community
Thanksgivings
67
75
107
124
129
136

II. Laments

A. Individual
3
4
5
6
7
9-10
11
13
16
17
22
25
26
27
28
31
35
36
38
39
40
42–43
51

| | | |
|---|---|---|
| 52 | 142 | III. Royal Psalms |
| 54 | 143 | 2 |
| 55 | | 18 |
| 56 | B. Community | 20 |
| 57 | 12 | 21 |
| 59 | 14 | 45 |
| 61 | 44 | 72 |
| 62 | 53 | 89 |
| 63 | 58 | 101 |
| 64 | 60 | 110 |
| 69 | 74 | 132 |
| 70 | 79 | 144 |
| 71 | 80 | |
| 77 | 83 | IV. Wisdom Psalms |
| 86 | 85 | 1 |
| 88 | 90 | 32 |
| 94 | 106 | 37 |
| 102 | 108 | 49 |
| 109 | 123 | 73 |
| 120 | 126 | 78 |
| 130 | 137 | 112 |
| 140 | | 119 |
| 141 | | 127 |
| | | 128 |
| | | 133 |

I have already indicated that form critics suggest psalms of a given type and structure likely derive from a particular setting. Most of the suggestions relate to worship. The scholar who has pursued this view more than any other is Sigmund Mowinckel. Mowinckel was a student of Gunkel, and he pursued his mentor's suggestion that the types of psalms originated in worship with an investigation of worship in ancient Israel and how the Psalms might relate to it. He came to the conclusion that psalms were used in worship, primarily in the Temple, and speak of actual worship activities. Mowinckel still operates from a form-critical approach, but his primary interest is the setting from which the Psalms arose, while Gunkel was primarily interested in the various types of psalms. Mowinckel sought the festivals or rituals from which a psalm came. We could describe his method as cult-functional along with Gunkel's type-analytical method.

I should pause to define the word "cult." By this term I do not mean some aberrant or abnormal faith or behavior. The term simply refers to the organized worship of ancient Israel, not exclusively but primarily in the Temple. This worship was central to the community's life. It helped the community understand its faith and embrace the ethical living central to ancient Israel's religion. Mowinckel defined worship as the visible and audible expression of the relationship between congregation and deity. The worship included word and visible acts, giving it a dramatic flavor.

The Psalms provided Mowinckel with many examples of worship language. The introductory call to praise in Psalm 105 uses action verbs:

- give thanks
- call
- make known
- sing
- tell
- glory
- rejoice

Worshipers today tend to think about those activities, while worshipers in ancient Jerusalem actually did them. The verb that begins verse 5 is also important: Remember. Mowinckel understood ancient Israel's worship to relate significantly to the history of the people. In worship they recited or rehearsed or enacted again and so remembered their story from the ancestral promise to slavery in Egypt to the Exodus to the journey through the wilderness and entry into the land of Canaan. Such a dramatic enactment enabled the history to live on in the community.

The Psalms exhibit other examples of worship experiences. Psalm 95 begins with a double call to worship. Imagine that the leader speaks the first call in the courtyard of the sanctuary.

> O come, let us sing to the Lord; . . .
> Let us come into his presence with thanksgiving. (vv. 1-2)

The people would respond by singing and processing into worship. The second call begins in verse 6, the call to bow to God their maker. The remainder of the psalm is a sermon or prophetic warning that the people should live out their faith.

Psalm 100 is often used as a call to worship in contemporary churches. The psalm leads worshipers to think about the significance of praising God, but in ancient Israel the language of the text reflected actions in worship. Note the actions mandated:

• make a joyful noise
• worship
• come into his presence with singing
• enter his gates with thanksgiving
• give thanks
• bless his name

When ancient Israel worshiped, the community enacted these imperatives. Entering God's courts with praise is to be taken literally with reference to the sanctuary

Psalm 26 provides a final example as a prayer for help. In verse 6 the worshiper speaks of washing the hands in innocence and going around the altar proclaiming the story of God's great deeds. Mowinckel again interprets those words as actual worship events in Jerusalem.

Part of Mowinckel's legacy of interpretation is to encourage readers to envision the language of the Psalms as a part of worship in ancient Israel. Ancient Israel's psalms were very much tied to the people's worship in word and deed. Their worship dramatized their faith so the current congregation could experience it anew. Mowinckel concentrated on the setting from which the Psalms derived and demonstrated that the setting was usually the preexilic cult in Jerusalem, and so the Psalms came from the community's worship life. Mowinckel took the work of Gunkel to its logical conclusion. The Psalms originated and were used in the cult.

The work of Gunkel and Mowinckel on the various types of psalms and their use in worship signaled a new beginning in scholarship on the Psalms. This form-critical approach to the Psalms stands in contrast to the way the Psalms were studied in prior centuries. That approach we might label personal/

historical. The task was to discover the person from whose life a particular psalm came, and the personal circumstances surrounding the composition provided the interpretive key.

In other cases, the issue was the historical event that gave rise to the text. For example, Psalm 6 appears to be a prayer of one who is sick. Various interpreters associated the text with the sickness of Job or of Hezekiah. On the historical side, Psalms 46 and 48 speak about attack on Jerusalem. Various interpreters have suggested that the attack led by Sennacherib and the Assyrian army in 701 B.C.E. provides the interpretive background for understanding the text. The difficulty with these interpretations of Psalms 6, 46, and 48 is that it is not really possible to specify with confidence the person or event from which the psalm came. Psalms 46 and 48 could allude to any attack on Jerusalem, and Psalm 6 could be the prayer of any sick person.

So the language of the Psalms themselves caused problems for the personal/historical approach in interpreting the Psalms. The language of these texts appears to be language that is representative of various people of faith. Therefore, it has been associated with a background in the worship of ancient Israel. I think we can thus see how scholarship moved to consider the types of psalms and their worship connections as important starting points for the interpreter. Gunkel especially saw this move in terms of bringing more objectivity to Psalms scholarship.

The form-critical approach to the Psalms has dominated scholarship in this century. It attends to the question of the structure and thus form or type or kind of psalm and its background in ancient Israel's worship, as opposed to questions of authorship and date. Mowinckel's reconstructions of ancient Israel's cult still carry much import in the world of Psalms scholarship, and I have already noted the impact of Gunkel's and Westermann's classifications of the Psalms. Most studies of the Psalms still begin with some type of classification.

These studies have had great impact on scholarship, but most of us are not engaged in scholarship at that level. What is the significance of all this talk about form criticism when you come to read the Psalms? Let me suggest several practical implications.

Many people find reading the 150 psalms in order to be confusing. A classification of the psalms helps with the questions of organizing a study of the Psalms. I suggest you read the Psalms according to the list of types in the classification chart. By reading this way, you can consider all the general hymns of praise or all the Royal Psalms together. You can also study Psalm 8 in light of the other Creation Psalms or Psalm 1 in light of the other Wisdom Psalms. This approach also reminds you to attend to the question of structure. We will see in the next chapter that the psalms of praise and prayer tend to have some typical structures, an understanding of which can help you grasp the movement of a psalm. Reading according to the classification approach also leads you to think not so much about who wrote the psalm when, but to consider its background in worship. As you read the text, try to envision what kind of worship service or prayer service this psalm could fit. If you want some information on those settings, read some Old Testament texts describing them (for example, Lev 23; 24; 1 Kgs 8), and consult commentaries or other works on the Psalms.

You may not be—or want to be—an ivory tower Old Testament scholar, but you can be an intelligent reader of the Psalms, and that can be one way you "love the Lord with all your mind." It will also intensify the impact of the Psalter in your faith pilgrimage. Our experience of public worship is also personal; the prayer and worship dimension of faith belong together. Any reader of a psalm thinks about its background because of references in the text and thinks about the movement of the psalm and what kind of literature it is. The text often reminds readers of other psalms. At some level, we all get at the concerns of form critics. Our discussion can help us be better and more purposeful readers of these texts and begin to see how these psalms relate to life. Attention to the kinds and movements and variety of psalms and their associations with worship provide a helpful beginning point for reading the Psalter.

## A Literary Approach

A form-critical approach to the Psalter provides helpful beginning points, but it is not the only beneficial way of reading the Psalms. Consider the approach I label "literary." In a sense, all approaches to the Psalms are literary; they all relate to this text, as a piece of literature. But there is an approach to interpretation that centers on the literary or poetic dimensions of these songs. In the last chapter, we noted the importance of Hebrew poetry. This approach extends that concern. The approach is akin to those that would study the literary qualities and devices in a Shakespearean play or in British poetry for example. Attention to such matters of poetic style can enrich our reading of the Psalter. While a form-critical approach focuses on what is typical in psalms, this literary approach gives more attention to the particular literary dimensions of the individual poems. In this section we will consider some background, examples, and suggestions for a profitable literary approach to the Psalter.

While attention to the literary qualities of the Psalms regularly has been part of the study of the Psalms, in recent years a number of scholars have reasserted the importance of a careful reading of the poetry. Probably the person most responsible for this emphasis is Robert Alter. He notes that poetry is a succinct, complex, highly structured, and rhythmical means of expression. We have already seen that the psalmists were part of the tradition of Hebrew poetry, but the psalms also exhibit a variety of poetic skills used to convey dramatic content.

A number of the recent studies on Hebrew poetry have concentrated on the nature of parallelism. The first chapter introduced the issue by describing parallelism as a kind of echo effect, which is a central part of Hebrew poetry. Others would suggest that such a description oversimplifies the matter. Still, we have noted that parallel structures, whether of words, phrases, lines or longer sequences of thought, are endemic to Hebrew poetry. The careful reader of these texts will keep the matter of parallel structures at the forefront and be attuned to the way words and lines are related in the Psalms.

Other poetic devices such as figures of speech and wordplay are also important as is the use of repetition. Alter also notes that many of the psalms grow in intensity and specificity as they move to a conclusion. The seeming simplicity of the Psalms can be deceptive. We would agree that the Psalms express deep and powerful faith. The poetic form provides the means of expressing such depth and passion. Attention to the artistry of the poetry can enliven our encounter with the text. We can more fully enter the faith being expressed and more fully appreciate it when we carefully attend to the movement of the texts, and especially its central turning points. These various studies emphasize the way in which a psalm persuasively creates and communicates its message.

What I have suggested about a literary approach so far indicates that we need to pay careful attention to the parallel structures or echo effects used in a psalm, and that we need to try to articulate the purpose for which a psalm uses language. When we study a story, we become aware of the plot as we read. In a sense, psalms also have a plot or at least a sequence that finally reaches a goal. I mentioned that these poems are structures of intensification; they move toward a goal. The opening lines of a psalm often give readers a clue as to the poem's purpose. It may be a plea seeking help in resolving a crisis, or it may be a call to praise seeking response from those addressed. Other psalms may relate to a task of faith. Many psalms conclude with some renewed call alluding to the opening section of the text and providing further evidence of its purpose. When we carefully read a psalm through its sequence or movement, we can begin to see how the poem uses language to achieve its purpose.

With that purpose in mind, I suggest that you ask four questions of a psalm. Reading a good, consistent, modern translation of a psalm can supply responses to the questions and begin the journey of interpretation. The questions can also lead to a deeper encounter with the psalm.

- How does the psalm use divine names?
- What words or phrases does the psalm repeat?
- How does the psalm use terms significant in the faith tradition of ancient Israel, terms such as "righteous" or "glory"?
- What figures of speech, such as comparisons or images, does the psalm use?

I have suggested that we read carefully a psalm, paying attention to any echo effects or parallelism in the poem and, with the help of the four questions listed, describe the purpose of the psalm. Some examples will illustrate the benefits of this literary approach.

Psalm 1 makes much use of parallels. It operates on the contrast between the righteous, described in the first part of the psalm, and the wicked, described in the last part of the psalm. The righteous are also compared to a tree that is rooted and nourished and so produces much fruit (v. 3). In contrast, the wicked are like chaff that gets blown away (v. 4). The final verse also emphasizes the contrast between the fate of the righteous and the wicked by way of antithetic parallelism.

> for the Lord watches over the way of the righteous,
> but the way of the wicked will perish. (v. 6)

The description of the righteous in verse 1 in terms of not walking, standing, or sitting suggests that the psalm is about lifestyles. The repetition of "wicked," along with the synonyms "sinners" or "scoffers," confirms the centrality of the contrast. The "righteous," repeated in verses 5-6, attend to God's law (v. 2). The text warns its readers to avoid the wicked and choose the righteous life. The psalm presents the contrast as a clear certainty. This brief example illustrates well how attention to the poetic artistry of a psalm can enrich our reading.

Psalm 100 is a familiar text to contemporary worshipers. It provides a good example of the significance of the divine name in a psalm. The divine name used is always the special Hebrew name for God, Yahweh, translated "the Lord." Each verse contains the name Yahweh except verse 4 where "his name" concludes the verse. Yahweh is clearly the subject of the praise, and the vocabulary of joy and thanksgiving permeates the text. The words of joy tumble on top of each other. The first two verses contain three lines, all of parallel thought:

- Make a joyful noise.
- Worship with gladness.
- Come with singing.

The concluding two verses of the psalm also exhibit parallel structures. In verse 4, we get the effect of four imperatives:

- Enter his gates with thanksgiving.
- Enter his courts with praise.
- Give thanks to him.
- Bless his name.

The last lines of the final verse speak in parallel ways of the Lord's constancy. This final verse uses two terms that are important in the Hebrew Bible: steadfast love and faithfulness. The two are often paired. Steadfast love refers to God's love, mercy, and grace. The term is sometimes translated "lovingkindness" or "unchanging love." Loyalty and constancy communicate something of the connotation. God's love does not change with external circumstances but continues. Faithfulness refers to God's truth or trustworthiness. History has shown God to be worthy of trust. God is the faithful one upon whom worshipers can rely. Note the image of the shepherd in verse 3, a reminder of God's benevolent care for the people. Also note that the psalm is closely associated with the sanctuary with references in verses 2 and 4. The Lord who made this people (v. 3) serves as shepherd and guide for this community. This psalm is a vibrant call to praise Yahweh in the sanctuary. The psalm then uses this powerful language for the purpose of getting a response from the hearers, a response of offering praise to God.

Psalm 13 provides a good and brief example of a different kind of psalm with powerful language. The text begins with the four-fold repetition of the question "How long?" The two lines of verse 1 are parallel, as are the three lines in verse 2, with the last line taking the thought to oppression from an enemy. Following the poignant questions in the first two verses, the speaker asks for help in verses 3-4 with the verbs "consider," "answer," "give light." It is also noticeable that the divine name "Yahweh" is used three times in this psalm, in the first and last verses and in verse 3 with a personal form of address, "O Lord my God," in the verse with the primary request in the prayer. These verses also articulate the consequences of divine inaction (death) as motivation for a divine answer. The pivotal turn in the psalm comes after verse 4, and the reader waits. The last two verses begin with "But I." The subject "I, myself, I" rejoices in the corresponding acts of Yahweh, "your steadfast love," "your salvation." The Lord has answered the plea and the conflict is resolved.

Psalm 101 is another example of a psalm with powerful language. The only occurrences of the divine name, both Yahweh, are in the first and last verses. The opening verse makes it clear that this song is a promise sung to Yahweh, and the frequent repetition of "I will" confirms that the text is a promise to the Lord. This psalm's language suggests that the text is about the speaker's lifestyle, with verbs such as "walk" and phrases such as "shall remain," "shall continue," and "morning by morning." The predominance of the first-person singular pronoun confirms that the psalm centers on the life of the speaker, but there is also a striking contrast between justice, with terms such as "loyalty, justice, blameless, integrity" in verses 1-2, and terms such as "evil, deceit, wicked, evildoers." This psalm uses a number of parallel lines to communicate a strong oath to bring about justice in the life of the speaker and of the community. Even this brief look at the language of the psalm provides important information for the reader.

The language of the Psalms is rich and artful, and so a literary approach to these texts can enrich our reading of them. Read them closely and carefully, giving attention to their poetic language—their parallelism, use of divine names, repetition, significant Old Testament terms, and figures of speech. Such tasks are not foreign to our reading. Be more intentional about attending to the Psalms' use of language in the journey toward articulating each text's purpose.

## A Canonical Approach

One of the recent concerns of some Old Testament scholars is that our interpretations not leave biblical texts locked in the past with no accessibility for contemporary readers. If we only attended to the use of Psalm 2 in ancient Jerusalem, our work would not be complete. So a number of scholars have begun to study how the book of Psalms came together. That would give some indication of what happened to the individual psalms after they were composed. These scholars agree that the Psalter we now have came to its final form long after the destruction of the Jerusalem temple in the sixth century B.C.E. Those who shaped the book read these texts in a setting rather different from the Jerusalem cult. For example, the Royal Psalms initially referred to the Davidic kings in Jerusalem. By the time the Psalter came to the form we now read, there was no king in Jerusalem. The community had come to see these texts as a testimony to hope for the coming messianic kingdom. Other Old Testament scholars have pressed forward to suggest that when we read the Psalms today, our primary context for reading is a context shaped by the book itself rather than a historical setting in ancient Israel. Thus we need to pay more attention to how the canonical book of Psalms is purposefully organized.

One of the scholars who has led this movement of attending to the canonical form of the Old Testament books is Brevard Childs. He emphasizes the concerns that seem to have been at the forefront when the book was organized. We can note several concerns that are important to the book as a whole.

- *Community Emphasis*—Many psalms are the words of an individual speaker, but in the book of Psalms, those texts are often put in the context of the whole community. Psalm 130 is a prayer from an individual but ends with a community emphasis. That is also true of the Psalter as a whole.

- *Hope for the Future*—Hope is a strong emphasis in the Psalms; Yahweh will bring deliverance. The laments consistently move from trouble to hope; the Royal Psalms also bear witness to hope for the future kingdom of God.

- *Influence from the Exile*—A particular example of hope for the future and community emphasis is also reflected in the Psalms. The Babylonian exile was a defining crisis for the Jewish community and caused them to view life differently. The suffering described, for example in Psalm 22, was applied to the suffering of the whole community in exile.

- *Language of the Psalter*—We have seen that the language of the Psalter is powerful; it is also language that is universally applicable and adaptable for life. It is open to use by many. The representative nature of the Psalter's language is one reason the book has held such significance through the centuries. The language can be used in a variety of settings. This type of language is also one reason the texts survived after the demise of the Jerusalem cult. The words of the Psalter could take on a broader interpretation as Scripture for the faith community. The language has a universal dimension to it.

- *Superscriptions*—The first chapter briefly described the super-scriptions attached to many of the Psalms. Several of the superscriptions associate a psalm with an event in David's life. These notes portray David not as glorious king but as repre-sentative person of faith. That kind of note can help readers envision the use of the psalm in a real life circumstance and in turn help readers see how the psalm could function in similar settings in their own lives.

- *Organization of the Psalter*—We also noted in the first chapter that the book of Psalms has been intentionally shaped as a collection. We noted that Psalm 1 introduces the book as *torah* (v. 2) for righteous living and that the book emphasizes a central dimension of that life's relationship with God, prayer. This introductory psalm then casts the book as divine instruc-tion as well as a prayer book. The concluding psalm of the book calls for a great gathering of praise, indicating that the life of righteousness the book has traversed has been worth the effort. The first part of the book is dominated by individual cries for help and the latter part of the book by community psalms of praise, indicating the parallel movement from individual to community and lament to praise.

The reason for enumerating these emphases is to give guid-ance to readers. When you are reading the Psalms, an awareness of these six items may help focus your reading, and your reading of the book will confirm their presence. The last emphasis of the organization of the Psalter is of further importance. Scholars such as Gerald Wilson and Clint McCann have suggested that the organization or sequencing of the psalms also provides guidance for readers. We have noted the significance of the introduction and conclusion of the book. Wilson also proposes that the first three of the five books of psalms relate to the Davidic covenant expressed in Psalm 2. In Psalm 89, at the end of Book III, that covenant comes to a traumatic demise. Books IV–V function as a response to the demise of the Davidic kingdom by affirming that from of old, long before the kingdoms of Israel and Judah, God was King for ancient Israel. These psalms reassert the kingship of God and provide a means for the faith community to move forward without monarchy or kingdom or temple. This way of thinking about the organization of the canonical book of Psalms provides another context for our reading.

At a very practical level, when we agree that the sequencing of the Psalms is purposeful, it behooves readers to think about the preceding and following psalms in the process of interpretation. Some illustrations might help clarify a canonical approach. When we read Psalm 61, we need to think about how it relates to Psalms 62 and 63, which exhibit language very similar to our text. Psalm 61 also relates to various canonical emphases enumerated above. Psalm 100 is a general hymn of praise, but it concludes a collection of psalms celebrating the kingship of God, and a Royal Psalm follows in Psalm 101. With these psalms on the kingship of God, the book begins the turn to praise spoken by the community. We have also noted that the first half of the Psalter is dominated by Davidic psalms, individual cries for help. Psalm 73 provides another interesting example. It is the first psalm of Book III and seems to come back to issues raised in the introductory Psalm 1. The speaker indicates that the prosperity of the righteous and the demise of the wicked had not been so clear. The conclusion the speaker derives, through worship, is that the presence of God is the ultimate good. This honest dialogue leads through the other Psalms of Asaph, building up to the demise of the kingdom in Psalm 89.

The full significance of a canonical approach to the Psalms has not yet come to the surface. Some contributions are clear, however. When you read the Psalms, give attention to the emphases of the canonical book enumerated above. Also think about where a particular psalm falls in the organization of the book and how the psalms before and after can help with interpretation.

## A Theological Approach

Many believers have read the book of Psalms with profit through the centuries, and they have done so without explicit attention to the type of psalm or its position in the Psalter or its background in worship or its poetic style. I have suggested that readers attend to these kinds of issues at some level, almost intuitively. But we have also noted the universal applicability of the language of the Psalms. Often a particular psalm appears to speak directly to the circumstances in the reader's life, a word of protest or comfort or thanksgiving. In those circumstances, readers do not think of how they are reading; the text interacts with life as they are experiencing it.

The efforts in this chapter to garner as much help as possible from the history of scholarship on the Psalms in order to improve our skills as readers should not in any way work against the kind of faithful reading of the Psalter I have been describing. Those who are serious about Bible study will be about a program of study. Then when they come to a crisis or celebration that leads them to the Psalter, their study will inform their reading out of a pressing need and enrich even more deeply the Psalter's word for them.

The kind of reading I have been describing is in tune with some recent study of the Psalter. It might be labeled a theological approach to the Psalms. In his *Praying the Psalms,* Walter Brueggemann talks about the necessity of allowing the language of the Psalms to interact fully with life. It is only when we allow the words of a psalm to enter into our experience that we come to the full impact of this life-centered language. The representative nature of the language makes that possible. Elsewhere Brueggemann constructs a typology of faith to organize a treatment of the Psalter. He speaks of psalms of orientation, disorientation, and new orientation.

The psalms of orientation are those that proclaim all is right with the world; life is oriented properly. Some of the psalms of praise and a number of the Wisdom Psalms would fit in this category. Psalm 1 with its clear delineation of the righteous life and its attendant prosperity and some of the Creation hymns with life properly constructed are examples. These texts resonate with the experience of readers when all is well.

Psalms of disorientation relate to those times when life has fallen apart; the proper orientation no longer holds. The lament psalms are the classic examples for this category. In Psalms 74 and 79 life has literally fallen apart for the community as Jerusalem has been destroyed. The speaker in Psalm 13 fears the onslaught of death. The language of these psalms expresses the chaos of experience.

With the psalms of new orientation, the hope of life has surfaced again but not in the same form as with the psalms of orientation. The experience of disorientation has brought a new awareness and vitality to life. The psalms of thanksgiving would be the classic examples here. Through the experience described in Psalm 30, the speaker comes to a new song. Psalm 107 speaks of joy after the experience of a variety of disorientations in the community. These psalms relate to the other side of crisis.

This cycle of orientation, disorientation, and new orientation describes the life of faith as suggested in the Psalter. I find this description of the relationship between the various kinds of psalms and the life of faith to be helpful in studying the Psalter.

The language of the Psalms is often immediately analogous to life experience. Many people have been comforted with the words of trust in Psalm 23. Those who encounter the loss of public life coming apart at the seams find that Psalm 137 gives shape to their anguish and enables them to continue moving through the experience. Those who have been besieged by all manner of evil have found words of hope in Psalm 13. The Psalms speak directly to the rawness of life, and our study of these texts needs to be attuned to that.

## Conclusion

At the beginning of this volume, I asked that we embark on a journey of reading and embracing the testimony of poets and sages. I then introduced the Psalter. In this chapter, I have described four ways of reading the Psalms.

- *Form-critical*—This approach operates on the basis of comparison and organizes the study according to the types of psalms. It also encourages attention to the structure of psalms and their background in worship.

- *Literary*—This way of reading emphasizes the poetic artistry of the psalm. Awareness of the style can help readers articulate the purpose of the text.

- *Canonical*—Here the question is how the psalm fits in the book of Psalms. How does it relate to those psalms before it and after it and to the overall structure of the book?

- *Theological*—This final way of reading begins from the relationship of the Psalms and life and seeks to foster that relationship. It encourages readers to allow the Psalms to interact with their experience.

The purpose of describing these ways of reading is to facilitate our journey. We can become more intentional about the ways we read. I believe that will help us become more intelligent and better informed readers and so will enrich our study of the Psalter.

This chapter draws from the history of scholarship on the Psalms. You may not be familiar with that kind of scholarship, but I have suggested that as readers we all attend to these issues at some level. We think about what we are reading and its movement and relationship to other, similar texts. We also think about background issues. We certainly notice literary devices in these poems and may well consider how a psalm relates to what came before and after it. In addition, we often relate the language of psalms to our life experiences. I propose that sharpening our reading and studying skills is an appropriate stewardship of our God-given abilities as people of faith and people of the book.

Much of the scholarship on the Psalms has concentrated on only one way of reading the Psalter. Unfortunately, few scholars take a multifaceted approach. The approaches are not mutually exclusive. These four, and others, all have contributions to make. This point does raise another issue, however. I am not suggesting that each time you study the Psalms you must follow each of these four approaches in order to be a responsible reader. Each approach or parts of an approach will be helpful at different times. Rather, I am suggesting that all of these ways of approaching the Psalter can be part of the bag of tools we carry with us on our journey of reading, and so this information will be available to us when we need it. Being attuned to our ways of reading can help us delight in, meditate upon, and seriously study this powerful book as testimony of poets, testimony that can deepen our life of faith.

## For Further Reading

Alter, Robert. *The Art of Biblical Poetry.* New York: Basic Books, 1985.

Brueggemann, Walter. *The Message of the Psalms: A Theological Commentary.* Augsburg Old Testament Studies. Minneapolis: Augsburg, 1984.

_____. *Praying the Psalms.* A PACE Book. Winona MI: Saint Mary's Press, 1982.

Childs, Brevard. *Introduction to the Old Testament as Scripture,* 504-25. Philadelphia: Fortress Press, 1979.

Gunkel, Hermann. *The Psalms: A Form-Critical Introduction.* Facet Books. Philadelphia: Fortress Press, 1967.

McCann, J. Clinton Jr. *A Theological Introduction to the Book of Psalms: The Psalms as Torah.* Nashville: Abingdon Press, 1993.

Mowinckel, Sigmund. *The Psalms in Israel's Worship.* 2 vols. Nashville: Abingdon Press, 1967.

Sheppard, Gerald T. "Canonical Criticism." In *Anchor Bible Dictionary.* Vol. 1, 861-66. New York: Doubleday, 1992.

Westermann, Claus. *Praise and Lament in the Psalms.* Atlanta: John Knox Press, 1981.

Wilson, Gerald Henry. *The Editing of the Hebrew Psalter.* Society of Biblical Literature Dissertation Series. Chico CA: Scholars Press, 1985.

# Chapter 3

# Prayer and Praise in the Psalms

Having attended to the shape of the book of Psalms and the approaches we take in reading the Psalter, we now turn more directly to the content of the Psalter. It will be impossible to consider all of the 150 psalms, and so we will study representative psalms with some broader comments about similar poems. The organization of this chapter is influenced by the classification of the Psalms discussed in the last chapter and particularly by the work of Westermann. He suggests that the Psalms move between the two poles of plea and praise, moving toward praise. We will thus begin with the plea side of the equation and the lament psalms. These psalms are cries for God's help in the midst of trouble, the most basic human cry. The cries come out of the very depths of human experience. Then we will journey on to the encounter with praise.

## Psalm 13 and the Lament Psalms

Psalm 13 is an ideal example of the prayers scholars often call lament psalms. They are not laments in the sense of a cry of resignation. Rather, they are laments in the sense of a cry to God for help. The laments have a fairly typical structure, an awareness of which can help readers move through the text.

- *Invocation*—the prayer is addressed to God (v. 1)
- *Complaint*—describes the crisis at hand and is sometimes called the lament section of the prayer (v. 2)

- *Petition*—the speaker cries out for help. In so doing, the speaker often gives reasons why God should help in the current crisis. (vv. 3-4)
- *Conclusion*—These psalms usually conclude in a hopeful way, perhaps with an expression of confidence or certainty that God will hear the prayer or a promise of praise. Some of the laments conclude with the praise itself. (vv. 5-6)

I caution readers not to take such structures as straightjackets that every lament follows. Rather, they are helpful heuristic devices to facilitate reading. Lament psalms were used in a variety of services in ancient Israel's worship during times when people were in crisis and sought divine help.

We have already given some attention to the poetry of Psalm 13. It begins with a series of four questions: How long, O Lord? God is nowhere to be found in the midst of the crisis at hand. The speaker's current experience is of trouble and of persecution from opponents rather than the blessing of God's presence. It appears that the speaker is close to death, and so a number of interpreters have suggested that the person is sick and has come to a prayer service to seek healing. But even in the midst of such pain, the cry is still to God, for ancient Israel believed that no matter what the crisis at hand, one was always in a position to cry out to God, even when it seemed the crisis was exacerbated by encountering the absence of a God who was supposed to be present. And yet when the speaker comes to the plea for help, the address is to "my God," indicating a relationship with God. The cry for help is that God will look and answer. Otherwise, the worshiper will die, and the opponents rejoice. The petition in verses 3-4 uses persuasive language in the prayer, suggesting God's reputation is in question. Should the opponents prevail, God's name as one who delivers will be in doubt.

With the last two verses, we encounter a sudden change of mood and an expression of certainty that God will deliver. Notice that this conclusion begins with the conjunction of contrast "but." This simple word is an important clue for readers of the Psalms; it means that a change is at hand. Now the psalm affirms that the speaker trusts in God and will rejoice in God's salvation and will sing to God. That is to say that salvation has been promised. Notice the last line "because he has dealt bountifully with me." The verb in this concluding line comes from the perspective of the one praying, and in that perspective, God's salvation is certain, but the rest of verses 5-6 suggest the deliverance has been promised and is yet to be fulfilled.

The conclusion of Psalm 13 is typical of many laments; they often come through the crisis at hand to a ringing affirmation of God's blessing and deliverance. This observation has led to the question of how this sudden change of mood has come to be. A number of scholars have suggested that between verse 4 and verse 5 the person offering the prayer in ancient Israel received a word from God, perhaps by way of a priest or other worship leader, a word promising deliverance. That explanation would fit a cultic background for psalms like this one but most of the texts do not indicate how the change of mood transpired. Other interpreters have left the matter to the characteristic movement of prayer from a person of faith. The tradition of ancient Israel taught that God delivers and perhaps the speaker came to terms with that teaching in the midst of trouble.

While it is entirely possible that the original speaker of this prayer was sick, the language of this psalm is adaptable for life. The prayer is one that any believer in real distress could pray. This kind of universally applicable language makes it difficult for interpreters to specify the circumstances from which the psalm originated, but the language enables contemporary readers to appropriate the words of the psalm as a prayer in life today. That comment moves us toward a canonical approach. Psalm 13 is part of the first book of psalms, a book dominated by cries for help from individuals. This text raises a variety of issues relevant to a number of the laments. It is impossible to comment on all of them, but let us take time to consider two

The first is the opponents or enemies in the Psalms. In Psalm 13, enemies appear to be part of the problem, though it is difficult to specify how they fit into the picture of the crisis at hand. The enemies appear to be waiting for the worshiper to fall; they are described like vultures circling over a prey nearly dead. The most striking thing about the enemies in this text is the enemy's disappointment. The movement of the text suggests that the enemies who are so oppressively present in the crisis will fade away, while God, who is so oppressively absent in the crisis, will become gloriously present. The enemies in the community laments are often national enemies of ancient Israel, but the enemies in the individual laments are described with such general and figurative language that it is difficult to identify them. On occasions the enemies appear to be those who exacerbate a crisis rather than cause it; perhaps the opponents perceive that the speaker, because of the crisis at hand, is suffering under divine judgment. So far as we can tell, these enemies are persons in the community of ancient Israel. They provide the opposition on which the plots of the psalms move.

The other matter worth consideration by way of Psalm 13 is the nature of the crisis at hand. I have suggested the possibility of sickness, but here and elsewhere the crisis is described in highly figurative ways. In many of the lament psalms, the crisis is described as a person's being constricted and choked and unable to breathe and live. It is as if the speaker is being choked to death. We might say that the person in crisis is gripped by the power of death that has invaded life. The sojourn in death gives rise to these profound cries for help. The hoped-for divine salvation would free the petitioner to a broad open place where life and breath and blessing are possible. The descriptions of crisis in the individual laments come no doubt from a variety of particular circumstances. Consider several possibilities, with examples.

- *Sickness*—The person prays for healing (Ps 6).
- *False Accusation*—The prayer is for a divine sign of acquittal. (Ps 7).
- *Malicious Gossip*—The person is accused but not in a legal sense (Ps 31).
- *Persecution*—In a number of the laments (ex.: Ps 55), the description of the crisis is quite general. In others (ex.: Ps 61), it appears that the speaker seeks protection in the sanctuary.

A number of the laments describe the crisis in such a general and figurative way that it is difficult to identify the problem in any meaningful way, though Brueggemann's category of "disorientation" is helpful.

A somewhat different way to think about the kinds of laments is dividing them into the categories of penitence and innocence. Some laments are prayers of penitence in the midst of guilt from sin, though the number is small. Psalm 51 would fit that label. More of the lament psalms could be called psalms of innocence, for example, Psalm 26, to which we now turn.

## Two Additional Laments

### Psalm 26

Psalm 26 is a prayer for vindication addressed to God. It emphasizes reasons why God should respond, an emphasis that is clear in the introductory plea.

> Vindicate me, O Lord,
> > for I have walked in my integrity,
> > and I have trusted in the Lord without wavering. (v. 1)

This first verse already indicates that much of the psalm is a protestation of innocence, probably in the face of some kind of accusation. The worshiper fears being counted among the wicked and so seeks a divine sign of vindication.

The poetry is artistic. Parallelism pervades the psalm. Note especially its use in verses 4-5. The text begins and ends with the divine name Yahweh, and repetition is particularly noteworthy. Frequent uses of the first person pronoun ("I" or "me") are balanced with the second person ("your"), indicating the relational dimension of the prayer. The text also underscores the innocence of the petitioner, in contrast to the wicked, seeking response with verbs of urgency: vindicate, prove, try, test, do not sweep away, redeem, be gracious. The repetition also includes a number of traditional terms from ancient Israel's faith to indicate the speaker's integrity and trust in Yahweh's steadfast love and faithfulness. At the conclusion of the lament, the petitioner is brought to a broad and level place, away from the constriction of the crisis and into Yahweh's favor. The central section of the psalm, verses 6-8, emphasizes the sanctuary as a place essential to resolution of the crisis at hand. The sanctuary is the place of the divine glory or presence and the symbol of divine refuge.

Hope and integrity are central to Psalm 26. The hope for the petitioner is found in relationship with God who is the final vindicator. This relationship is nurtured in worship and lived in integrity. These important lessons the psalm teaches for communities of faith. Also important to note is the honesty of the dialogue in this psalm. Much of contemporary Protestantism is dominated by prayers seeking forgiveness; this prayer seeks vindication. In honesty and integrity, the worshiper protests to God seeking divine justice. The prayer is a bold address to God.

## Psalm 137

Psalm 137 provides a parade example of the honest dialogue of faith. This psalm is one for which readers can readily imagine a historical background. In the sixth century B.C.E., the Babylonian armies marched into Judah and conquered the nation including its capital Jerusalem. The city was left in ruins. Those who were of influence were taken as captives to Babylon. This defeat constituted the destruction of the world as the ancient Israelites had known it and so brought much trauma for the community. Our psalm opens with a poignant scene among those in exile from Jerusalem/Zion. Zion had been known for its worship and its psalms, but now is in ruin.

The next verses move toward a response to the traumatic state of exile—in an idolatrous place. The first response is memory; the vow is to remember Zion and Jerusalem and its songs. Then the call is for God to remember those who perpetrated the destruction, Babylon and the Edomites who aided in the defeat. The conclusion of the psalm is a harrowing cry for vengeance on the Babylonian oppressors:

> Happy shall they be who pay you back
> what you have done to us!
> Happy shall they be who take your little ones
> and dash them against the rock! (vv. 8-9)

The hope is that conqueror Babylon will now be defeated. These verses may be the most horrific example, but this feature of the cry for vengeance is in other psalms. Understandably, many readers simply ignore these psalms as distasteful and contrary to the teachings of Jesus. At the same time, these texts can contribute to a holistic view of faith. The speakers seek justice for those who have been wronged, and they operate from the perspective of God's people. They understand themselves to be speaking out against the enemies of God.

It is also important to remember that these psalms are prayers to God. They do not advocate violence against enemies but plead with God to bring about the vengeance that is the Lord's. It is thus possible to see such prayers as liberating acts of faith. The lamenter describes the crisis and places the matter with God who is the final arbiter. God will decide, and the psalms plead for God to decide against the enemies. This psalm and the Psalter as a whole are remarkably honest in the dialogue with God.

The psalmists knew long before the advent of modern therapy that for communities and individuals to deal with pain and anguish, the pain and woe must first come to expression. Psalm 137 cries out from the ruins; a way of life is no more. Perhaps the prime example of such a psalm from an individual is Psalm 109. The speaker suffers under the assault of "lying tongues" and has become an object of "scorn." The articulation of such pain enables the individual or community to move forward and deal with it. One deals with anguish, anger, and pain by working through it rather than going around it. And take note that these cries are cries addressed to God. All of this "negative" part of life is included in the honest dialogue of faith. The saints of old did not hold within grudges, anger, or pain, but brought them to expression in prayer.

Psalm 137 is also an example of a community lament. While there are fewer community laments than individual laments, both categories partake of similar structures and moods. The community laments speak of crises harming the nation: military defeat, famine, societal corruption. These psalms are more dominant in the last half of the Psalter.

The largest single category of psalms in the Psalter is the laments. In fact, it is probably not wise for a reader to attempt reading all the individual laments on one occasion; pain might ensue. It is important to see, however, that in these prayers the trouble and woe of life are included in the context of relationship with God, the "I-Thou" relationship. God has risked a covenant relationship with ancient Israel and in many of the lament psalms, the speakers insist that God bring that agreement to bear in the midst of crisis. The laments are thus bold and honest prayers, calling for God to act in the midst of trouble and woe. The lamenters wrestle with God. Such honesty in relationship with God is foreign to many contemporary people of faith and as a result, we often miss the depth of faith found in these prayers. In the Psalms, one can never move beyond dialogue with God. Even in the profound anguish of Psalm 88, the speaker is still addressing God. The faith in the laments is a bold one, crying out of the very depths of human experience. And the concluding affirmation of these prayers is that God hears.

## Psalm 30 and Prayers of Thanksgiving

Up to this point, our discussion of prayer in the Psalter has hovered around the pole of plea. It should have already become clear, however, that those pleas are on the way toward the other end of the spectrum, the pole of praise. The laments cry out to God in the midst of crisis and often conclude hopefully, sometimes with a promise of praise. The psalms of thanksgiving are positioned after the crisis has passed and fulfill the promise of praise by offering thanksgiving to the God who delivers. As with the laments, there are thanksgiving psalms spoken by individuals and by the community. The two share a typical structure and many additional common features. Psalm 30 provides a good illustration of the structure.

- *Introduction*—The opening section announces the intent to give praise and thanksgiving to God (vv. 1-5).
- *Narrative*—The body of the text describes the crisis (vv. 6-7), the prayer for help (vv. 8-10), and the deliverance (v. 11).
- *Conclusion*—The psalm ends with a renewed promise of praise (v. 12).

The worship setting for such psalms is a service of thanksgiving, perhaps including sacrifice; Psalm 118:21 describes the background:

> I thank you that you have answered me
> and have become my salvation.

The crises from which the speakers have been delivered are described in the same way that the laments describe crises. The speaker has been gripped by the power of death, but God has brought about deliverance, and so the worshiper narrates or declares the deliverance in worship so others can see God's work. The specific crises are quite similar to those in the lament psalms.

In Psalm 30, the introductory verses declare the intent to praise the God who has delivered the speaker from the power of Sheol. Sheol is the realm or world of the dead, the underworld, and psalms often picture Sheol as a power that can invade life and become manifest in the kinds of crises we have already seen. The speaker was gripped by the power of Sheol but here announces the intent to offer praise and thanksgiving to God and invites the congregation to participate, for God has delivered from the jaws of death. Verse 5 well illustrates the poetic description of joy.

> For his anger is but for a moment;
>     his favor is for a lifetime.
> Weeping may linger for the night,
>     but joy comes with the morning.

Beginning with verse 6, the speaker tells the story of this sojourn. The worshiper was on top of the world and all of a sudden, things fell apart (v. 7). In the midst of trouble, the worshiper cried for God to help, seeking to persuade God with the desire to live and continue to bear witness to God's faithfulness. With verse 11, readers hear with the striking image of God's turning mourning into dancing and sackcloth into joy that God has delivered. Sackcloth was the customary Hebrew dress in times of mourning and distress. Now joy is the order of the day because of God's deliverance. The concluding verse renews the promise of praise and thanksgiving.

Prayers of thanksgiving are essentially testimonies. Westermann calls them psalms of narrative or declarative praise. They narrate the story or declare to the congregation the story of how God has delivered from a specific crisis and so encourage faith among those present to hear the story. The praise these psalms offer is thanksgiving for deliverance from trouble. They provide a link between the poles of plea and praise and speak of genuine hope for the faith community. The Psalter moves in that direction, and a number of the community thanksgiving psalms are in the latter half of the Psalter. As the speakers have moved from death to life, so the readers of the Psalter also move from the power of death to the power of life. Psalm 34:8 typifies these psalms' exuberant thanks.

> O taste and see that the Lord is good;
> happy are those who take refuge in him.

## Psalm 117 and the Hymns of Praise

The psalms of thanksgiving exhibit a praise that narrates God's deliverance from a crisis. That praise is associated with a broader praise Westermann calls descriptive; it describes God in more general terms and is probably the kind of praise readers most often associate with hymns. This sort of praise is well illustrated with the shortest psalm in the Psalter, Psalm 117. This psalm would have been one of the hymns of praise offering adoration and praise to God as part of ancient Israel's worship. The hymns also exhibit a typical structure.

- *Introduction*—The hymns begin with a call to praise (v. 1).
- *Body*—The body of the psalm gives the reason(s) for praising God (v. 2).
- *Conclusion*—The conclusion of the hymn is a renewed call to praise, often similar, if not identical, to the opening call to praise. The last line of Psalm 117 is like the first.

Central to the structure is this practice of giving reasons for the praise of God. The style is present in many of the hymns, and attention to the pattern can be helpful to readers.

Psalm 117 begins with a version of the word "Hallelujah," praise the Lord. The term is two words in Hebrew: "Hallelu" is a plural imperative call to praise, and "jah" is a shortened poetic form for the special Hebrew name for God, Yahweh. So the psalm opens with a call to praise Yahweh, and the call is a universal one, for all nations and peoples to glorify God.

The first word of verse 2 is important. The Hebrew term means "because" and introduces the reason for praising God. The body of the hymns of praise characteristically provides reasons for praising God, and the hymns do so in a variety of ways. Some describe God with relative clauses, the God who delivers or the God who heals. Others use participles, such as God the saving one or God the blessing one. Yet others use titles or epithets: God as shepherd or strong refuge or savior.

Frequently the hymns will introduce the body of the psalm with the Hebrew word translated "because" or "for" as in Psalm 117. Why should the community praise Yahweh? The reason is that God's steadfast love and faithfulness are ever working for the people. We have already looked at this important Hebrew word pair when considering Psalm 100. History has shown that God is worthy of trust and has demonstrated that God's loyalty to the community is ongoing. Praise is the proper response to the experience of God's great constancy and trustworthiness.

The psalm then concludes with the renewed call to praise, "hallelujah." "Hallelujah" is, in a sense, the central part of a hymn of praise in the same way that "how long?" is central to the laments. And so we have moved from "how long?" to "hallelujah," the two poles of plea and praise. The Psalms attend to both and all points in between as part of the pilgrimage of faith.

The hymns of praise came from a variety of worship settings in ancient Israel, offering adoration to God as part of the worship experience. One way to think about the variations on hymnic praise is to consider the reasons given for praising God.

The thanksgiving psalms narrate one reason: God delivers from crises. The general hymns of praise more broadly recount the history of God's saving the people. Psalm 105, for example, recounts this history from the ancestral promise to entry into the promised land. Other hymns call for praise of God as creator and sovereign of the created order. Psalm 8 offers a familiar word of praise. It varies the hymnic form with identical introduction and conclusion that, rather than calling for praise, immediately speak the praise. God has created strength out of weakness, and the speaker delights in the night sky as well as the wonder of the place God has given humans in the created order. The psalm reflects on the created order in the tradition of Genesis 1 and then comes to the concluding word of praise. Other hymns celebrate the presence of this creator and ruler with the people in Zion. We have already noted Psalms 84 and 122, which rejoice in the divine presence as pilgrims journey to worship in Jerusalem/Zion. Psalms 15, 24, 46, and 48 all celebrate the divine presence on the temple mount as a refuge and hope for the faithful. This God who is present with the people also instructs the people with prophetic words in Psalms 50 and 81. And finally, the trustworthiness of God comes through in the psalms of trust such as Psalm 121 or the familiar Psalm 23.

## Two Additional Hymns

### Psalm 23

The twenty-third psalm is certainly the most familiar for contemporary readers. The psalm describes Yahweh as shepherd in the midst of crisis.

> Even though I walk through the darkest valley,
> I fear no evil;
> for you are with me;
> your rod and your staff—they comfort me. (v. 4)

This imagery suggests that a crisis of some type is in the background of the psalm though it is difficult to describe it in any detail. The latter part of the psalm associates the prayer with worship, and so I have chosen to consider the psalm along with the hymns that praise God as trustworthy shepherd, though the psalm certainly departs from the typical hymnic pattern and does relate to some kind of crisis.

The most-noted image in the text is that of God as shepherd, and the beginning of the psalm considers the image during the risky time of changing pastures. The shepherd guides and comforts and leads the flock to life, even in the face of threats, even in the face of the deepest darkness, traditionally translated "the valley of the shadow of death." The shepherd renews life. In the last two verses of the psalm, the shepherd serves as host. God provides table and oil, which are symbolic of joy in the face of threats from enemies. This experience of refuge is so powerful that kindness rather than enemies will now pursue the worshiper.

The conclusion of the psalm ties the experience of trust to worship in the sanctuary. Faith communities throughout the generations have found hope in the midst of trouble in this psalm and rightly so. The text in stirring poetry evokes the image of Yahweh as trustworthy giver of life in the midst of trouble and woe. The text thus nurtures faith among believers and paints a vivid portrait of faith as part of the praise of God in worship. The drama the hymns put before the community of faith is the call to praise. Will the community respond? The texts then give reasons why praise is appropriate. One reason is the trustworthy shepherding God accomplishes, and the power of poetry like that in Psalm 23 coaxes worshipers to respond in praise.

## Psalm 98

Another important emphasis in the hymns of praise is Yahweh's rule over the creation. This reason for praising God is celebrated in the enthronement psalms, most of which come in a collection of Psalms 93–100. These hymns call for praise to Yahweh in a new song because Yahweh the creator continues to rule over the creation. These psalms reflect a joyous time of worship, perhaps in the fall festival times in ancient Israel, and they confront the community again with the majesty and sovereignty of God.

Psalm 98 is a good illustration of an enthronement psalm. The psalm operates on the hymnic pattern of the call to praise and reasons for praise, but the pattern runs throughout the text rather than exhibiting a clear introduction, body, and conclusion. The opening call to praise is to sing a new song, followed immediately with a rationale.

> O sing to the Lord a new song,
>     for he has done marvelous things.
> His right hand and his holy arm
>     have gotten him victory. (v. 1)

The language refers to the great victory of the Exodus, and that victory was public for all to see. The victory bears witness to God's relationship with ancient Israel and demonstrates God's "steadfast love and faithfulness," a word pair we regularly encounter in the Psalter. The exuberant call to praise is renewed in verses 4-6 with the imagery of musical instruments. This middle section of the psalm begins as does Psalm 100, the hymn of praise concluding this collection of enthronement psalms.

The call to break forth into joyous praise calls for the use of melody and song, the lyre, trumpet, and horn.

> With trumpets and the sound of the horn
>     make a joyful noise before the King, the Lord. (v. 6)

The concluding verses of the psalm move the call to praise into creation. The call is for the sea, the world, the floods, and the hills to sing for joy. The key to this imagery is in the first line of verse 9, "at the presence of the Lord, for he is coming. . . ." At the advent of God, any and everything is possible, even for the sea and the hills to give praise to the king of the universe. Furthermore, the expectation is that the king will bring righteousness and justice to the creation.

Psalm 98 is a good illustration of the praise of Yahweh as ruler, and in this particular text as the ruler who delivers. That affirmation brings hope and thus the call to sing a new song, which is characteristic of these enthronement psalms. Psalm 98 interacts with the narrative of the Exodus and from that act of deliverance moves to the expanse of all creation. It is an artful piece of poetry, beginning with the victory and drawing its readers into joy and praise by way of music and the creation. The advent of King Yahweh brings change and right relationship with the creation. At the beginning of the psalm, God brings victory and a place for ancient Israel. That reality is expanded to the nations at the conclusion of the psalm. Such an affirmation of praise offers much hope to communities of faith.

The "Book of Praises" moves toward the praise of God, implying that the life of faith moves in the same direction. The first part of the Psalter is dominated by lament; praise becomes the dominant note of the second half. Much of this turn comes with the new song of the enthronement psalms. The Psalter then concludes with a great exclamation of praise:

> Let everything that breathes praise the Lord!
>     Praise the Lord! (Ps 150:6)

The language of the hymns of praise moves in two directions. It offers praise to God, and it calls the community to praise. With the use of vivid imagery and the sense of tradition in ancient Israel, with the use of powerful poetic artistry, these texts urge the community forward to the praise of God. And the texts continue to bring joy and refreshment for communities of faith.

Our consideration of the prayers of the Psalter glimpsed a vivid portrait in the the shadow of God's absence. The descriptive hymns of praise round out the portrait with the joys of the presence of God. God grants wholeness of life, and the community rejoices. The community gives thanks for deliverance and gives voice to the broader praise of God as creator and redeemer. The hymns of praise vibrate with the practice of the active presence of God.

The psalms of praise also provide a significant model for the praise of God. How does one praise God? The psalms recount what God has done and how God has been present. They narrate and describe God's involvement in the world. So when the community praises God, it bears witness to God's presence and activity. The words of praise also serve to deepen the faith of the community and invite all into the jubilant praise of God. As with the lament psalms, the psalms of praise are also vivid and honest. The praise is uninhibited because of genuine delight in the goodness of God. And all of this jubilation carries real depth. Remember that there is always a reason to praise God. There is real substance and richness to the praise of God in the Psalms. The hymns bear witness to a bold faith in the God who delivers and blesses and thus is to be fully praised. As such these hymns nurture faith at the core of the community's life and worship.

## Psalm 2 and the Royal Psalms

Our journey of reading has taken us through much of the prayer and praise of the Psalter, but there is yet more. Two other smaller groups of psalms bear some distinctives from those we have been considering. The first is the Royal Psalms. Strictly speaking, the Royal Psalms do not make up a literary category. The texts include a variety of literary forms with the common denominator of relation to the Davidic king in Jerusalem. The king was central to the life of ancient Israel and central to its faith. For that reason, I continue in the tradition of Gunkel to give separate consideration to these psalms. These texts relate to a variety of settings in the life of the king: preparation for battle, a royal coronation, a royal wedding. We will consider Psalm 2 as a way of entry into these texts.

Psalm 2 consists of four sections, the first of which describes the plotting of rebellious vassals (vv. 1-3).

> Why do the nations conspire,
>> and the peoples plot in vain? (v. 1)

Yahweh's response to such a prospect is but laughter (vv. 4-6). Then the king whom Yahweh has established on Mount Zion speaks, beginning in verse 7, and recounts the divine declaration on this the day of royal coronation. God has decreed that the Davidic king is now Yahweh's adopted son and is established to rule. The final section (vv. 10-12) calls the "rulers of the earth" to submit to Yahweh's authority. This first royal psalm probably came from a coronation ritual in Jerusalem. At a vulnerable time, the text declares a divine guarantee for Davidic rule. God has made a covenant with David that the Davidic line will rule over the people in Jerusalem, and so rebellion against God's anointed only brings grief. Such an emphasis would have been familiar in the ancient Near East and been part of royal rituals used in the courts of the region, as would the custom alluded to in verse 9.

> You shall break them with a rod of iron,
>> and dash them in pieces like a potter's vessel.

With the scepter, the king smashes a pot to indicate the fate of those who rebel against God and God's anointed. And so the psalm concludes by encouraging kings to give allegiance to God and the Davidic line.

It is noteworthy that this psalm's articulation of the Davidic covenant promise comes at the beginning of the Psalter. By the time we reach Psalm 89, that promise has come to an untimely demise, and the latter parts of the Psalter affirm instead the kingship of Yahweh, which was the basis of the affirmation in Psalm 2. We have already seen the links between Psalm 2 and the introductory Psalm 1. Psalm 2 offers for nations the same choice urged in Psalm 1, the life Yahweh offers in contrast to the death that comes with rebellion against the author of life. The intentional placement of this royal psalm indicates that it has application beyond the narrow confines of the Davidic line in preexilic Jerusalem. The text offers sure hope of the coming kingdom of God and calls communities to allegiance to the only giver of life. The striking images in this text affirm that view of the psalm. The picture of the rebellion, God's response in laughter and fury, and the smashing of the pot powerfully remind hearers/readers of God's sovereignty. The structure of the text also supports such a view. The first and last sections speak of Yahweh's authority while the second and third speak of God's choice of the Davidic monarch. Behind the Davidic line is the divine authority.

## Wisdom Psalms

A final group of psalms will provide transition to the next chapters in our journey, the wisdom psalms. These psalms originate from the circles of wisdom teachers who also penned the book of Proverbs and seek to pass on wisdom for living the life of faith. These texts communicate in forms characteristic of the wisdom books treated in the remainder of this volume. The texts emphasize several themes:

- Reverence for God and "torah" (ex.: Ps 119)
- Contrast of righteous and wicked (ex.: Pss 73; 112)
- Instruction in daily living (ex.: Ps 133)

We have already noted that the introductory Psalm 1, a wisdom psalm, is based on the contrast between righteous and wicked. Psalm 37 well illustrates the outcomes of these two lifestyles. In righteous, wise living is found blessing; in wicked, foolish living is found difficulty. The wisdom psalms seek to inculcate the life of wisdom for the faith community.

> Trust in the Lord, and do good;
>> so you will live in the land, and enjoy security. (v. 3)
>
> The wicked plot against the righteous,
>> and gnash their teeth at them;
> but the Lord laughs at the wicked,
>> for he sees that their day is coming. (vv. 12-13)
>
> For the arms of the wicked shall be broken,
>> but the Lord upholds the righteous. (v. 17)

These verses raise the question of the prosperity of the wicked, a theme of importance in the wisdom books as well. These psalms ask such questions that are explored in greater depth by the sages in their own books. This glimpse at the wisdom dimension of the Psalter whets the appetite for what is to come.

## Conclusion

Our journey of reading through the Psalter has been brief but should give us a feel for the various kinds of psalms in this treasure of faith. Our journey has described the honest dialogue of faith, from all parts of the faith pilgrimage. All of life is lived in relationship with God, and the dialogue of faith relates to all of life. The context for such dialogue is the worshiping community. Just as our reading of the Psalms is a journey, so the community of ancient Israel was on a faith pilgrimage through life. These psalms are their songs for that trip. They are honest, exciting, amazing, and demanding in their praise of God and cries to God, texts that are central to the biblical witness. The witness of these poets nurtures our honest dialogue of faith for the way. I hope these glimpses of the Psalms will encourage and enliven your reading of these beautiful and powerful resources for the life of faith.

Chapter 4

# What Is Wisdom?

Most of us can probably quote a few proverbs and say something about the story of Job, but if we are honest, few of us know much more about the books usually tied to the sages or wisdom teachers in ancient Israel: Proverbs, Job, and Ecclesiastes. For a variety of reasons, Old Testament scholars in this century have also participated in ignoring these books until recently. Primary attention has gone to those books associated with covenant theology and the Exodus deliverance, seen as the dominant emphases of the Hebrew Scriptures, emphases that are not strongly present in the wisdom books.

As some have begun in recent years to see the importance of wisdom in the whole of the Old Testament as well as the pervasiveness of some of the theological emphases of these books, scholars have begun to attend more to these books and their significance. For most of us, however, the major problem is that we simply do not know much about the wisdom books of the Old Testament. I hope the following chapters can begin to remedy that problem. Our journey will begin with background material that can help us understand the books and then deal with each book in order: Proverbs, Job, Ecclesiastes.

## Wisdom in the Old Testament

To gain an understanding of wisdom in the Old Testament, it will be helpful to begin by putting Proverbs, Job, and Ecclesiastes in the context of the Old Testament and its sociohistorical setting. In this way, we can see the importance of wisdom for

Old Testament faith. The Hebrew canon contains three main divisions: the Law, the Prophets, and the Writings.

The Law or torah consists of the Bible's first five books. Scholars who study the first chapters of Genesis have begun to see that as these texts reflect on the beginnings and significance of human life as well as human freedom and responsibility therein, they portray various wisdom emphases. Especially is that so with the search for knowledge in the Garden in Genesis 2–3. The character Joseph in the latter chapters of Genesis was also a wisdom character or sage. He partook of divine wisdom and interpreted dreams and effected sound administration. Connections between the wisdom in Proverbs and much of the legal material in this first section of the Bible has also been noticed.

The Prophets section includes the books of the Former Prophets (Joshua, Judges, Samuel, Kings) as well as the Latter (Major and Minor) Prophets. The Court History of King David includes wisdom teachers as well as reflection on the nature of wise leadership. King Solomon was famous for his wisdom. Various of the Latter Prophets have also been associated with wisdom. Recent studies of Amos, Micah, and Isaiah have especially noted ways these prophetic books interact with wisdom teaching.

When we come to the Writings, wisdom is already prevalent in Job, Proverbs, and Ecclesiastes, and we have noted the presence of Wisdom Psalms. Like Joseph, Daniel was in some sense a wisdom figure who interpreted dreams and taught with insight.

These brief comments make it clear that wisdom is not limited to the three books most often associated with the sages but is one of the significant dimensions of the social and religious life reflected in the Old Testament. As there were prophets and priests and kings, so there were sages, and each functionary brought to bear the emphases of his or her office in the life of the faith community ancient Israel.

## Wisdom in the Ancient Near East

Ancient Israel was not alone in having wisdom teachers as part of a culture. Most of the ancient Near Eastern nations had scribes, and a number of wisdom texts from those cultures have been unearthed. The Old Testament narrative describing King Solomon's rule alludes to the wisdom of the East and especially to the wisdom for which Egypt was known. Ancient Israel's wisdom then was part of a broader cultural wisdom movement, and we need to consider that background when studying the wisdom books.

The Egyptian wisdom texts are generally of two types. A number of the texts give practical, everyday advice for living. The advice often attends to proper behavior in the pharaoh's court. The other texts are much more speculative and concerned with the deeper meanings of life. They often reflect on the order of life and its importance for living. I mention one particular Egyptian text, the Wisdom of Amenemope that is often compared to Proverbs 22:17–24:22. There are many similarities, and most Old Testament scholars would suggest that the writer in Proverbs was aware of Amenemope's work.

Awareness of these broader ancient Near Eastern wisdom texts suggests that the pursuit of wisdom was an ancient practice long before ancient Israel came on the scene. Wisdom is a universal reality available to the whole of creation. The broader search for wisdom in the ancient Near East provides the socio-historical setting out of which the wisdom books come. They did not appear suddenly from heaven without a cultural background; rather they reflect a historical background, as we have seen with the Psalms and more generally the Old Testament.

This background and the search for wisdom therein becomes the medium of God's revelation in these books. One of the important theological implications of the cultural background reflected in the wisdom books is that it shows God was actually involved with those people in that particular time and place. God did not remain aloof from their life and history but instead effected self-revelation in a way clearly present to their life together. The broader canonical and cultural contexts of wisdom lead to more particularities.

## The Vocabulary of Wisdom

"Wisdom" as a term is used in a variety of ways in the ancient Near East, with the goddess of wisdom or with wisdom gained in age or in study. It also is associated with a variety of skills and understandings. Intelligence, knowledge, and insight are all part of what we have been calling "wisdom." The Egyptian word most often used is *Ma'at*, usually associated with the order of creation and one's participation in that order. When we narrow our attention to the Old Testament, we also find a variety of terms used to denote wisdom, but the primary term is *hokmah*, which is especially associated with teaching and instruction. It also is associated with the insight that comes with age and with righteousness. The righteous life is a wise one. The opposite of wisdom is folly or foolishness, and the seat of wisdom is the heart. Most contemporary readers think of the heart in terms of emotion, but in Hebrew the emotions were more associated with the bowels. The heart was the seat of intellect or will or wisdom. The Hebrew term can have a variety of meanings:

- *Skill*—Exodus 28:3 speaks of those with ability or skill in sewing to produce priestly garments for Aaron. The term used in both cases is the one for wisdom. One can be a wise and, thus, skillful seamstress or farmer or teacher.

- *Cleverness*—Jonadab is characterized as very crafty or clever in 2 Samuel 13:3; the term used is "very wise."

- *Magic*—The language of wisdom is used in the book of Daniel in association with the magicians of the Babylonian court.

- *Encyclopedic knowledge*—The first chapters of 1 Kings speak often of Solomon's wisdom; he is the paradigm of the wise king. First Kings 4:33 especially emphasizes encyclopedic knowledge as part of Solomon's wisdom.

- *Intelligence*—The wisdom of Solomon includes intelligence, which is probably the sense of the term in Jeremiah 9:23.

- *Practical advice*—The prologue to the book of Proverbs (1:2-6) speaks of the purpose of the book as passing on basic advice or wisdom for living.

- *Moral Discernment*—King Solomon's wisdom also includes moral discernment, emphasized in 1 Kings 3 (see v. 9).

- *Reverence for God*—In Proverbs 1:7, wisdom is associated with the fear of the Lord or reverence for God. The "fear" is not physical fear but reverence or respect and thus obedience to God. In the first chapters of Proverbs, wisdom is also personified as Woman Wisdom who calls people to learn of the wisdom God can give.

This list is in no way exhaustive, and a variety of the connotations may be present in various texts and times. Still, this brief list suggests the various understandings the vocabulary of wisdom holds.

## The Nature of Wisdom

The history of scholarship reveals various attempts to craft a cogent definition of wisdom in the Old Testament. Gerhard von Rad, a scholar of a generation ago, suggested the empirical knowledge of order as the Old Testament's basic understanding of wisdom, and that emphasis has continued to influence students of these books. There is order in creation and in society, an order related to justice and righteousness. Learning wisdom is gaining this empirical knowledge of order for the purpose of succeeding in life. Note the connection to the Egyptian notion of *Ma'at*. Von Rad was also aware of the limits of wisdom, especially in the book of Ecclesiastes, and added that human ability to cope with reality and its ambiguity are also part of the goal of the wisdom teachers. So for von Rad, wisdom relates to both the order and meaning of life and faith and the mystery of life and faith.

Two contemporary American scholars, James Crenshaw and Roland Murphy, have sought to refine von Rad's work. Crenshaw speaks of wisdom in terms of a quest for self-understanding. The sages search for how life fits together in the world of nature, society, and theology. They see the order and chaos of creation and seek to relate that to human experience. Murphy also suggests that the wise seek to relate human conduct and nature. He understands wisdom as the effort to establish order. The contemporary British scholar Norman Whybray has suggested a much broader understanding of wisdom as the intellectual tradition of the Old Testament. The sages are simply those asking the basic questions about life, and what surfaces in the wisdom books is the common store of sense for life.

Despite these efforts, the exact definition of wisdom in the Old Testament continues to be something of an enigma. I believe, however, that we can note some characteristics of wisdom and then attempt a tentative definition that has implications for helping us understand the wisdom books.

- Wisdom comes from observation. One experiences life and, in so doing, gains wisdom for teaching.
- Wisdom is connected with morality or justice. The sages encourage the living of the good, moral life. How social ethics relate to the practical details of life is important to the sages.
- Wisdom comes from God. God knows the way to wisdom.
- Wisdom functions like Torah. It teaches the life of faith.

So we might define wisdom as a way of describing the divine-human relationship in terms of seeking to understand the orderly processes of life and living by them. The wisdom teachers then seek to pass on this understanding. Observation, then, is the method of the wise, and, having learned, they seek to pass on wisdom in the context of the teacher-learner relationship. Undergirding this understanding of wisdom is a creation theology. When God created the world and life and provision for life, God also placed wisdom in the creation. God continues to bless life, and part of that blessing is enabling people to find wisdom for living. Such a discovery issues in wholeness of life. In Proverbs, Job, and Ecclesiastes, the sages are passing on such wisdom.

The Old Testament contains essentially two types of wisdom. Proverbs typifies the first, practical or pragmatic wisdom for daily living. The second kind of wisdom is speculative wisdom, which is primarily in Job and Ecclesiastes. These books speculate about or reflect on central issues in life. They often revolve around questions rather than answers. The poetic books of Proverbs, Job, and Ecclesiastes then seek to pass on wisdom for the life of faith. Imagine that you wanted to bequeath words of advice about life to your younger siblings or children, and you will have a reasonable sense of what the sages are doing.

## The Setting of Wisdom

We have attended to the nature and language of wisdom as well as its setting in the Old Testament and broader culture. What about the social background of wisdom more specifically in ancient Israel? The origins of wisdom in ancient Israel are somewhat shrouded in mystery, but essentially two possibilities have been proposed: the royal court and the family or clan.

Gerhard von Rad suggested that literature and culture began to flower around the royal court, especially in the time of Solomon. He even speaks of a "Solomonic Enlightenment" and associates the beginnings of wisdom with Solomon's relationship with Egypt. Crenshaw suggests that the traditions associating Solomon with wisdom are more of the legendary type tied to his wealth as a monarch. Crenshaw ties the origins of wisdom further back to the popular circles of clan and family. R. B. Y. Scott has preferred an association with Hezekiah rather than Solomon. There are other variations, but the two primary suggestions are court and family.

I would suggest that Solomon's court was important for the place of wisdom in ancient Israel. By the time of Solomon, the kingdom was flourishing in Jerusalem, and the bureaucracy required educated people. Teachers and schools would have been part of this establishment, and it is likely that passing on wisdom would have been part of the task. Proverbs 25:1 suggests that the schools were continuing in Hezekiah's day. It is entirely possible that the tradition of passing on wisdom to the next generation was part of family tradition in ancient Israelite society, but I suspect that custom was institutionalized around schools in Jerusalem during the monarchy. This wisdom movement began rather early in the kingdom but came to full flower rather late in ancient Israel.

Ancient Israel had four kinds of leaders: king, priest, prophet, sage. Kings and priests came to their position through inheritance, prophets through divine call, and sages by way of education. In the time of the kingdoms, kings were ascendant followed by priests and prophets. After the fall of the kingdoms, priests and sages rose to positions of greatest influence.

The Old Testament supports the view that Solomon was the patron of wisdom in ancient Israel, the one who gave the initial impetus and authorization for it to flourish in Jerusalem. Several texts in Kings support that view. First Kings 4:29-34 and 5:12 speak of Solomon's wisdom. Chapter 10 puts the visit of the Queen of Sheba in the context of wisdom, and 1 Kings 3 describes Solomon's reign in terms of wisdom. The king's association with Egypt and with biblical wisdom books also supports this view. So while a family setting for wisdom is not to be discounted, the more likely background is in schools associated with the royal court beginning in Solomon's day. There is little textual evidence for schools in Jerusalem during the monarchy, but on analogy with ancient Near Eastern evidence, they probably existed.

The background of wisdom in ancient Israel and the ancient Near East as well as the Old Testament along with an understanding of the nature and language of wisdom should help guide our journey through the wisdom books. We begin with Proverbs.

## For Further Reading

Bergant, Dianne. *What Are They Saying about Wisdom Literature?* New York: Paulist Press, 1984.

Crenshaw, James L. *Old Testament Wisdom: An Introduction.* Atlanta: John Knox Press, 1981.

Morgan, Donn F. *Wisdom in the Old Testament Traditions.* Atlanta: John Knox Press, 1981.

Murphy, Roland E. *The Tree of Life: An Exploration of Biblical Wisdom Literature.* The Anchor Bible Reference Library. New York: Doubleday, 1990.

Perdue, Leo G. *Wisdom & Creation: The Theology of Wisdom Literature.* Nashville: Abingdon Press, 1994.

Von Rad, Gerhard. *Wisdom in Israel.* Nashville: Abingdon Press, 1972.

Scott, R. B. Y. *The Way of Wisdom in the Old Testament.* New York: Macmillan, 1971.

Whybray, R. N. *The Intellectual Tradition in the Old Testament.* Beihefte zur Zeitschrift für die alttestamentliche Wissenschaft. Berlin: Walter de Gruyter, 1974.

## A Framework for Reading the Wisdom Books

*Proverbs*

- Reverence for God underlies all maxims, even though not explicitly stated.

- The proverbs are understood as part of the instruction for honoring God and finding life.

- No premium is placed on failure, indolence, stupidity, mediocrity, tactlessness, and friendlessness. The wisdom teachers value the opposite.

- Wisdom is not automatic; it needs to be learned. Proverbs are thus often pithy condensations of years of experience.

- Wisdom celebrates life. There is little of disease, suffering, problems. It may seem simplistic (in Proverbs), but it is guidance that represents tendencies.

*Job and Ecclesiastes*

- Job is partly a reaction against a simplistic understanding of Proverbs. It is concerned with how will and should a person react if all his/her values are removed. How can life be worthwhile when that happens?

- Job protests against popular royal wisdom that humans cannot control life. It suggests that if there is any inner reason to life, it is known to God alone. Job is not the model of the patient sufferer, the stoic. His deep rage at the distresses that assail him comes across in a thundering majesty of rhetoric. His is a mighty rage. He asks angry questions and waits for an answer. God responds, "None of your business!" Life is in God's hands, not ours, so we are to put our faith in God.

- Ecclesiastes footnotes that there is control in life, but suggests that it is a control of seasons and rhythms whose inner workings humanity cannot know.

# Chapter 5

# Proverbs
# Wisdom for Full Living

One of the most helpful considerations for understanding the book of Proverbs is to reflect on the function of a proverb. The Hebrew term for proverb is *mashal*, the basic meaning of which has to do with comparison. This term is also the background for Jesus' parables in the New Testament; Jesus often compared the kingdom of God to a variety of things common to life in his day. Proverbs often trade in comparisons in order to instruct in daily living. They are compact and memorable sayings of practical instruction. They might be called a teaching sentence about living fully. We use such sayings in our day: Like mother, like daughter. Parents instruct children in how to behave when guests come. Teachers instruct small children in how to behave in the cafeteria. The sayings are applicable to daily living.

The book of Proverbs contains sayings of various types. The following list is not exhaustive but gives some indication of the variety.

| Type | Examples |
|------|----------|
| Comparisons | 16:8; 27:15 |
| Similitudes | 25:11; 26:11 |
| Observations | 16:18 |
| Paradoxes | 27:14; 29:5 |
| Opposites | 27:7 |
| Characteristic Behavior | 10:18; 20:4 |

A proverb, then, is a brief, pungent teaching sentence. It offers concrete, cogent advice for living. This description of the literary form makes it clear that the collection of proverbs would be characterized as practical wisdom. The nations surrounding Israel also produced proverbs in the universal search for wisdom for abundant living. In the Old Testament, these proverbs are a gift from God, a gift of teaching that comes from observing life and the created order. The sages seek to pass on to the next generation what they have learned about life.

## Background

The book of Proverbs is the primary Old Testament example of practical or pragmatic wisdom. It offers wisdom for daily living. Some background information on authorship, date, and setting should facilitate our journey through the book.

### Authorship

Traditionally, Solomon is designated as author of the book, and with reason. Consider the following evidence:

- "The proverbs of Solomon son of David, king of Israel" (1:1)
- "The proverbs of Solomon" (10:1)
- "These are other proverbs of Solomon that the officials of King Hezekiah of Judah copied" (23:1)

Elsewhere we find different headings, however, for example,

- "The words of the wise" (22:17)
- "These also are sayings of the wise" (24:23)
- "The words of Agur son of Jakeh. An oracle" (30:1)
- "The words of King Lemuel. An oracle that his mother taught him" (31:10)

These headings in the text of Proverbs suggest that it is not really accurate to say that Solomon wrote the book of Proverbs. The book is a collection of proverbs from various sources. At the same time, we have already seen the strong connection between Solomon and the Old Testament's wisdom tradition. I have little doubt that Solomon wrote Proverbs, but I interpret the headings "proverbs of Solomon" to indicate a grouping of proverbs collected under the royal, Solomonic patronage. Solomon was the initial patron of wisdom and of the use of proverbs. He was, I suspect, instrumental in bringing together many of the proverbs in the book, but it is clearly an oversimplification to say that Solomon wrote Proverbs. No doubt, the tradition of royal patronage of wisdom continued in Jerusalem.

## Date

The fact that the book is a collection also has a great impact on the matter of date. The various proverbs come from a variety of times and places. We have already seen the heading in 25:1 that indicates the collecting of this group of proverbs during the time of Hezekiah. The book came together over a period of time. Most of the sayings are probably preexilic, but it is difficult to know when the book reached its canonical form. That probably happened after the exile; fifth century B.C.E. is a reasonable surmise.

## Setting

Two possible settings apply for Proverbs. Some of the sayings may have originated in family or clan settings with the older generation passing on wisdom for living to the younger generation. I have already suggested that the royal court in Jerusalem was a pivotal setting for the sages. I suspect that many of the proverbs were assembled by sages in such a context, as indicated in 25:1. Their purpose was a teaching one, to pass on advice for full living. Such a social background for the book suggests that it was shaped by members of the Jerusalem establishment who were at the higher end of the socioeconomic scale in ancient Israel. The optimistic view of life in much of Proverbs reflects that setting.

## Structure

Proverbs is organized for the most part by collections. An outline follows.

  I. The Book's Purpose (1:1-7)
 II. The Call to Wisdom (1:8–9:18)
III. Solomonic Proverbs (10:1–22:16)
 IV. The Sayings of the Wise (22:17–24:34)
  V. Solomonic Proverbs (25:1–29:27)
 VI. Sayings of Agur (30:1-33)
VII. The Words of King Lemuel (31:1-9)
VIII. The Good Wife (31:10-31)

The book begins by calling its audience to learn wisdom that is personified as Woman Wisdom who calls people to learn. The book's sayings instruct the young based on the sages' observations of life and creation. Learning to live fully requires effort. The sayings in Proverbs provide content for the necessary learning. Proverbs are poetic in form and so center on the parallel structures of Hebrew poetry as described in chapter 1. At times Proverbs that use a particular kind of parallelism, especially antithetic parallelism, seem to be grouped together.

## Proverbs and Theology

Central to the message of Proverbs is the description of two lifestyles: wise and foolish. In the wise or righteous life, one encounters good; in folly, one finds trouble. The contrast between the lifestyles and their consequences is pivotal for the book. It is important to remember that these sayings present tendencies or generalizations about full living. They are not to be read as an attempt to cover every detail of life. A contemporary road sign will illustrate.

When a driver comes to a dangerous curve and the sign says 15 miles per hour, it means that the driver's best chance to navigate the curve successfully will be at a speed no greater than 15 miles per hour. A poor driver might crash even at the speed of 10 miles per hour, or a daring driver might make it around the curve at 22 miles per hour. But the sign still stands as wise counsel for driving. A maximum speed of 15 miles per hour is the best policy when going around this curve.

Take the illustration to the consequences of the wise and foolish life. The perspective of proverbs is not like unto a vending machine in which one deposits good acts and receives a set reward in return or deposits foolish ways and gets a set judgment in return. Rather, in living wisely, most likely one will encounter abundance of life; in living foolishly, one will see trouble. Proverbs do not intend to cover every small detail in life. What characterizes a style of life is at issue.

Also important for reading Proverbs is the warning that these sayings are not intended to be read backwards. For example, Proverbs 22:6 says, "Train children in the right way, and when old, they will not stray." That proverb is not intended to make parents whose children get into difficulty feel guilty or as a test to find good parents. Only the parents of model adults qualify. Rather, the proverb offers a word of hope for parents. Responsible parenting is the best way to prepare children for a productive future. Proverbs 6:10-11 provide another example.

> A little sleep, a little slumber,
>> a little folding of the hands to rest,
> and poverty will come upon you like a robber,
>> and want, like an armed warrior.

This saying does not mean that all poor people are lazy or that all wealthy people are conscientious. Some are given wealth and do nothing; some work hard and remain poor. The proverb opines that the best way to a productive life is diligence.

These examples illustrate that the book of Proverbs presents practical, orthodox observations on successful living. Undergirding these observations is the creation theology summarized in the last chapter. God placed wisdom in the creation and enables teachers to find the orderly processes of life and teach them. Proverbs passes on such wisdom about living. The book is a call to full living according to such wisdom. Proverbs 8:35 says that whoever finds wisdom finds life; Proverbs 11:19 takes a similar view. Proverbs is a call to life.

## Content

### Proverbs 1–9

Perhaps we have covered enough background information to take a look at the text of Proverbs. The first nine chapters of the book serve as an opening section that introduces the other collections of proverbs. After the opening heading, verses 2-7 of chapter 1 articulate a teaching purpose for the whole book. Learning wisdom is equated with righteousness and justice in verse 3. In verses 4-5, groups of people are specified as the audience of the book. The simple and the young are parallel. The simple are those who are yet to learn the way of full living. But the wise and the discerning can also learn from the book. They will herein learn to interpret proverbs and other images as well as other sayings of the sages.

The final verse of this brief prologue to the book states the motto of the book.

> The fear of the Lord is the beginning of knowledge;
> fools despise wisdom and instruction.

The basis and starting point for wisdom or knowledge is reverence for God. The contrast is to the opposite of a wise person, the foolish person who rejects any instruction or learning. That contrast between wisdom and learning and folly is fundamental to Proverbs. This introductory verse also makes the fear of God a basis for what follows in the book. The maxims are often not explicitly theological, but this introduction puts them in that context. This verse and the whole opening prologue affirm the purpose of the book as the teaching of wisdom. A number of scholars have suggested that chapters 1–9 were prefixed to the already existing collections of proverbs, but in the final, canonical book these opening chapters provide a framework for reading the book.

The remainder of the first nine chapters continues to emphasize the call of wisdom to learn of full living. The next verses speak of passing on wisdom to the next generation, and the remainder of chapter 1 warns about the connection between morality and relationships. The advice of the wicked will lead astray. Wisdom, on the other hand, calls to wholeness of life. Proverbs 1:20-33 personifies Woman Wisdom as calling the naive and unknowing to learn; therein is life. The warning is that rejection of learning leads to death. Chapter 2 finds many images to articulate the value of wisdom for a healthy life. Much of the language in the chapter is akin to the normative faith tradition of ancient Israel ("commandments, justice, righteousness"). The last verses of chapter 2 introduce another contrast important to these first chapters, the adulteress who leads astray in contrast to Woman Wisdom who leads to life. The term "loose woman" may suggest connections with idolatry.

The benefits of wisdom continue to come to the surface in chapters 1–9. Wisdom is connected with abundance (3:1-12), but the gaining of wisdom is more precious than wealth (3:13-18). Note the connection between wisdom and creation in 3:19-20. Relationships are central in wisdom's view of life. Living a wise, upright life brings honor.

> The wise will inherit honor,
> > but stubborn fools, disgrace. (3:35)

Repetition is a teaching device used in Proverbs. Chapters 4–5 continue with the twin themes of all sorts of enticements to persuade readers to embrace wisdom along with warnings to reject the opposite, the adulteress. The parent or teacher addresses the child or learner.

Two of the hallmarks of wisdom sayings show up in chapter 6. In verses 6-11, an example from nature, the ant, becomes a way to encourage diligence in living. A numerical proverb is in verses 16-19.

> There are six things that the Lord hates,
> > seven that are an abomination to him. (v. 16)

Seven evils are then listed as representative of one who has been enticed by folly.

Chapter 7 describes a scene as a kind of parable about a young person who has not yet gained wisdom, a naive youth who is enticed by the adulteress we might call "Dame Folly." She seduces the youth like a prostitute. She entraps him in folly, in evil that leads to Sheol, the realm of death. The contrast moves into chapter 8 with wisdom's noble call to learning and true wholeness of life. Wisdom is again connected with faith, reverence for God (v. 13), and abundance in life.

With 8:22, this opening section of the book reaches its high point in describing creation through the eyes of Woman Wisdom. Wisdom was the first of the creations and there as God's delight in all the acts of creation. The poet calls on the creation traditions of Genesis to emphasize the importance of

Wisdom. Wisdom was built into the creation from the beginning and now calls people to learn of this wisdom God has implanted in creation.

> For whoever finds me finds life
> and obtains favor from the Lord;
> but those who miss me injure themselves;
> all who hate me love death. (8:35-36)

Wisdom prepares a feast to entice those who need to learn wisdom, the fear of the Lord, which leads to completeness in life. In contrast is the garish seduction of Dame Folly, which leads to death.

Proverbs 1–9 demonstrate the connection between wisdom and creation and the call of Woman Wisdom to come and learn. The call is to learn the way of wisdom and so avoid the deadly way of the wicked, the way of folly. The personification of wisdom as a woman is important in these chapters. Some scholars have interpreted Woman Wisdom as the remnants of an ancient Near Eastern goddess brought into the Hebrew fold or as a manifestation of God or as simply another image. It seems best to stick with the notion of personification.

In Proverbs, wisdom is described as a woman calling people to learn. Woman Wisdom is close to God, and is God's delight and beside God at creation (8:30) and enters the creation as God's messenger calling people to learning. Wisdom is a proclaimer and revealer of reverence for God as a way to full living. Woman Wisdom is a "person" from God speaking to the creation. In Wisdom, a woman, God reveals the way of life and relates to humanity.

These introductory chapters form a kind of theological and practical poetic essay that introduces the collections of proverbs to come. Wisdom teaches of everyday life and of faith. Proverbs teaches wisdom, and in these opening chapters, Wisdom calls readers/hearers to learn. I have already suggested that wisdom came to its fullest flowering after the exile. Ron Clements has suggested that wisdom as the fear of the Lord was especially important after the destruction of the temple. It enabled the people dispersed to keep their faith without the temple cult. They could still practice reverence for God in whatever place or circumstance they found themselves. Proverbs 8 also provides the wisdom background for the prologue to the Fourth Gospel: "And the word become flesh . . ."

### Proverbs 10:1–22:16

With this theological and pragmatic context in mind, we come to the collection of Solomonic proverbs that forms the core of the book. They appear almost as a series of pearls strung together in a sparkling necklace. It would be impossible to consider all of the sayings. I have chosen Proverbs 11:1-11 to illustrate the chapters. I encourage you to read the text and outline your response. These verses are classic illustrations of the proverbial form—brief, pungent sayings about full living. Most of these proverbs also partake of antithetic parallelism, as evidenced by the contrast between the two lifestyles, wise and foolish, and their theological dimensions.

The wise are passionate about full and just living and contribute to the community in a hopeful way. They celebrate and enjoy the life they have been given and seek to follow the priorities of righteousness. They seek to live in sync with the created order. Their lives are characterized by integrity and truth.

The foolish ones, in the book of Proverbs, can be those who are without wisdom but can learn. In other cases, they are brainless wonders who have been seduced by folly, thick-skulled and crude scoffers who arrogantly distort the truth. They shamelessly turn good to evil. They provide a negative example in Proverbs 11. Their injustice can destroy a community, but their downfall brings rejoicing (v. 10). Verse 10 is a good illustration of the function of a proverb. It does not instruct the righteous to rejoice at the perishing of the wicked but rather observes that the downfall of the wicked brings joy to the community. The community depends on the integrity and contribution of the wise and faithful. This text illustrates many of the themes readers will find in this middle section of Proverbs.

James Crenshaw has described the teaching on life and wisdom in Proverbs in terms of the pursuit of knowledge. Self-control in all of life is essential to wisdom. Consequently, certain behaviors are to be avoided: adultery, drunkenness, laziness, gossip. Such behavior characterizes the foolish and leads to destruction. Wisdom calls people to fullness of life and reverence for God. Proverbs is about moral formation in ancient Israel. This central collection of wisdom maxims is important for that task.

### Proverbs 22:17–31:31

Proverbs 22:17 begins two collections that take the heading "Sayings of the Wise." The first of these is often described in terms of Egyptian influence, especially from the Wisdom of Amenemope. The sayings continue to be concerned with character formation for the young. A significant concern for Proverbs is that those growing to maturity will "seize the day," take advantage of the opportunities, from God, to live fully.

> Do you see those who are skillful in their work?
>> they will serve kings;
>> they will not serve common people. (22:29)

This concern with the royal court continues in the beginning of chapter 23.

> When you sit down to eat with a ruler,
>> observe carefully what is before you,
> and put a knife to your throat
>> if you have a big appetite. (23:1-2)

These sayings are explicit in giving instructions to inexperienced courtiers. When one dines with royalty, one is modest in consumption. The concern again is educating for making the most of every opportunity in life. There is still a concern for justice and the perspective that there is much more to life than wealth. Wisdom is the crowning glory of life; it brings hope and a future. The contrast between the wise or righteous and the foolish or wicked is still at the fore.

> Do not lie in wait like an outlaw against the home of the righteous;
>> do no violence to the place where the righteous live;
> for though they fall seven times, they will rise again;
>> but the wicked are overthrown by calamity. (24:15-16)

The instruction of the Wise commends the life of righteousness; it survives even the complete experience of trouble. Seven is the number for completeness. The instruction in this section is consonant with what we have seen previously. The concluding saying of the second collection of the Sayings of the Wise repeats a maxim encountered in Proverbs 6:10-11 put in a slightly different context. Here the speaker tells a kind of parable from what has been observed. The lesson again is to be diligent in living to the fullest.

> I passed by the field of one who was lazy,
>> by the vineyard of a stupid person;
> and see, it was all overgrown with thorns;
>> the ground was covered with nettles,
>> and its stone wall was broken down.
> Then I saw and considered it;
>> I looked and received instruction.
> A little sleep, a little slumber;
>> a little folding of the hands to rest,
> and poverty will come upon you like a robber,
>> and want, like an armed warrior. (24:30-34)

Proverbs 25–29 contain an additional collection of Solomonic proverbs. The sayings tend to be a little longer in chapters 25–27, and they give further instruction in daily living. Proverbs 26:27 is a clear illustration of the moral order built into creation, in the view of the sages.

> Whoever digs a pit will fall into it,
>> and a stone will come back on the one who starts it rolling.

Evil committed returns upon one's own head like a boomerang. This moral order is worked out everyday in relationships. The saying at the conclusion of chapter 27 again shows the concern that the wise take advantage of the opportunities from God to live fully.

> Know well the condition of your flocks,
>> and give attention to your herds;
> for riches do not last forever,
>> nor a crown for all generations.

> When the grass is gone, and new growth appears,
>> and the herbage of the mountains is gathered,
> the lambs will provide your clothing,
>> and the goats the price of a field;
> there will be enough goats' milk for your food,
>> for the food of your household
>> and nourishment for your servant girls. (27:23-27)

The concern for justice continues to be front and center.

> If a king judges the poor with equity,
>> his throne will be established forever. (29:14)

The last two chapters of Proverbs are somewhat different. The Sayings of Agur are rather enigmatic. The first fourteen verses of chapter 30 appear to be a kind of dialogue in which the speaker raises a number of questions about ever knowing wisdom. The speaker seems to question the moral order of life. Beginning with verse 15 is a series of numerical sayings, as illustrated in verses 21-23.

> Under three things the earth trembles;
>> under four it cannot bear up:
> a slave when he becomes king,
>> and a fool when glutted with food;
> an unloved woman when she gets a husband,
>> and a maid when she succeeds her mistress.

When the created/social order is overturned too radically, chaos ensues.

Proverbs 31:1-9 recounts three points of advice to King Lemuel from his mother:

• Beware of women.
• Avoid strong drink.
• Defend the rights of the needy.

The concluding poem of Proverbs (31:10-31) is an alphabetic acrostic, that is, each verse begins with the next letter of the Hebrew alphabet. The poem is about the good wife, who is described very much as the wise person. She is diligent in contributing to family and community; she demonstrates her wisdom in life. She is a wise teacher, "a woman who fears the Lord," perhaps also an example of Woman Wisdom to conclude the book. This good wife is another call to wisdom and a model for how to incarnate it.

## Conclusion

In Proverbs we find the sages' primary example of traditional, orthodox wisdom. Here the sages observe life as God created it and pass on their observations as pragmatic teaching on the tendencies of life. Ancient Israel heard a variety of voices— prophets, priests, kings. It was important also to hear the contribution of the wise teachers. Their sayings provide realistic instruction for daily living, with the conviction that all of life is sacred because it comes from God. They fully embrace a moral order to life, bequeathed by the creator, with the contrast between wisdom and folly at its center. So the sages commend living the full, wise life; therein is the crown and joy of humanity.

## An Exercise

Read the following texts from Proverbs and try your hand at interpreting them: 6:6-11, 12:6, 13:10, 20:15, 28:5. Consider the following questions/tasks in your interpretive work.

- What type of proverb is the saying? What type of poetic parallelism does it use?
- Paraphrase the saying.
- Define key words.
- Consider the context, that is, the sayings before and after the text.
- How does the saying relate to the characteristics of wisdom discussed in chapter 4?
- How does the saying relate to the broader faith tradition of the Old Testament?

## For Further Reading

Clements, R. E. *Wisdom in Theology.* The Didsbury Lectures. Grand Rapids: Wm. B. Eerdmans Publishing, Co., 1992.

Crenshaw, James L. *Old Testament Wisdom: An Introduction.* Atlanta: John Knox Press, 1981.

_____. "Proverbs, Book of." In *Anchor Bible Dictionary.* Vol. 5, 513-20. New York: Doubleday, 1992.

# Chapter 6

# Job

# Wisdom in Dialogue

The introductory look at wisdom in chapter 4 suggested that there are two types of wisdom books in the Old Testament, practical and speculative. Our journey revealed the book of Proverbs as the primary example of practical or pragmatic wisdom. We now come to the books of Job and Ecclesiastes as examples of speculative wisdom. These books speculate or raise questions about life. First is the book of Job. Job is a book of great literature and drama and one that has attracted much interest through the centuries. It has also exercised considerable influence on literature and drama. Crenshaw mentions the work of MacLeish, Jung, and Goethe; Murphy mentions Kierkegaard, Chesterton, Gutiérrez, Frost, and other commentators. In this chapter we will consider first a number of background issues and then take the journey of reading through the book.

## Background

### Plot

I. Prologue
   A. The Setting (1:1–2:13)
   B. Job's Lament (3:1-26)
II. Three Cycles of Poetic Speeches
   A. Who Is God? (4:1–14:22)
   B. The Wicked Person (15:1–21:34)
   C. Job Is Sinful (22:1–31:40)
III. Elihu's Speeches (32:1–37:24)

IV. The Divine Speeches
 A. Speeches from the Whirlwind (38:1–40:2; 40:6–41:34)
 B. Job's Responses (40:3-5; 42:1-6)
V. Epilogue (42:7-17)

The book of Job begins by introducing Job as the blameless and upright man who fears God and turns away from evil. The scene quickly shifts to the divine throne room where the council of the Lord is meeting with the Satan in attendance. A question is raised about the blameless character of Job, and a challenge to Job's faith results. Job is struck with all manner of troubles, including a loathsome disease in a second round of trouble. At this point, three of Job's friends make the journey to come and comfort him. Then Job speaks a powerful lament out of his trauma.

With chapter 4, three cycles of poetic speeches begin. Each of Job's companions—Eliphaz, Bildad, and Zophar—makes a speech, and Job responds to each. Six speeches comprise each cycle. In the first cycle, Eliphaz, Bildad, and Zophar describe God as one who punishes the wicked, and Job maintains his innocence. The speakers often talk past each other in these dialogues. In the second cycle, the three visitors imply that Job is somehow wicked and so has brought this trouble on himself. That perspective comes to a head in the third cycle. Job begins to see that the answer to his crisis lies not with these visitors but with God who is the real issue. Job makes a final plea followed by a hymn to wisdom. Job's protestation of innocence concludes the third cycle.

The next chapters witness the sudden appearance of Elihu to set the record straight. He indicates that Job's suffering serves a disciplinary purpose. These speeches help with the transition to the divine speeches from the whirlwind, speeches about the wonders of nature. Job does not respond to the first speech, but after the second, agrees that he has claimed more than he should and submits to God.

The book concludes with the restoration of Job. We will return to the plot in more detail, but this summary will be useful in exploring several introductory issues.

## Composition

Scholars have raised a number of questions about how the book of Job originated. One of the first things readers notice is the distinction between the prose framework in the first two chapters and epilogue and the poetic parts of the book in between. Often it has been suggested that the prose and poetry had different origins. For example, some scholars suggest that the ancient story of Job has been supplemented with the poetic dialogue in order to explore additional wisdom issues. Apparently, Job was part of the tradition in ancient Israel (Ezek 14:14). A number of scholars have noted the tensions between the prose and poetic parts of the book. The characterization of Job is different in the two parts as is the type of religious practice. Sacrifice is important in the opening scene; dialogue is primary in the poetry, which also uses different names for God. Some have suggested that Job 19:17, which speaks of Job's family, is in conflict with the introduction in which his children die, but there could be other members of Job's family. The restoration of Job in the epilogue also takes a different perspective than the poetic dialogue, but the two can still stand.

An honest reader will agree that there are tensions between the prose frame and the poetic sections of the book, though some of the differences may have been exaggerated. It is also the case that a narrative framework is needed to provide a setting for the poetry. If we read the book of Job as a drama and see the characters in that light, we can read the book as a coherent whole. That is the most constructive route. The prose and poetry may have originated at different times, but that need not deter our journey of reading.

Scholars have also raised questions about the Elihu speeches. Elihu appears abruptly without any mention elsewhere and with no replies to his words. At times these speeches appear to be commenting on the rest of the book. Because they are of a different style and poetry, many have suggested that they have been added to the book. Even so, these chapters serve a function in the book. We will explore those issues later, but at this point, it is fair to say that Elihu's speeches are part of the transition to the divine speeches that follow. Scholars have also suggested that the hymn to wisdom in Job 28 is an addition along with various other sections. We will consider the textual problems at the end of the third cycle of speeches when we attend to those chapters. I conclude by saying that the book of Job is probably a composite book. Nonetheless, it has come to a final canonical form that offers a coherent text fruitful for the journey of contemporary readers.

## Date

When was the book of Job written? That is a different question than the question of when the character Job is pictured as living. Job is pictured as a patriarchal figure, but most agree that the book came from a much later time. The book tells the story of this legendary character but gives no explicit date, and so we are left to construct the book's setting and propose its date. Based on the language and theology of Job as well as its place in the wisdom tradition, most scholars suggest that the book came together during the time of the Babylonian exile or after. A sage brought together this powerful document in a time when the issues it treats were front and center because of the suffering of ancient Israel in the fall of the kingdoms and resulting exile.

## Literary Form

The book of Job takes the form of a wisdom dialogue. Claus Westermann suggests that it is rather an extended lament psalm. Certainly there are elements of lament in the book, but dialogue is the more relevant umbrella form. The book exhibits great eloquence. It uses many poetic devices: irony, rhetorical questions, repetition, allusion, analogy, various images, anticipation, and plot movement. The book is a powerful read.

## Setting

The context in which we read Job will have an impact on our interpretation. In his commentary on the book, Norman Habel suggests that we read the book as an expression of the universal human dilemma of suffering. It certainly is the case that there are various Job-like documents from other peoples in the ancient world. There is even a document sometimes called the Babylonian Job, a dialogue between a righteous sufferer and a visitor. Of course, any document has its distinctives. In the Babylonian document, the dialogue partners come to the conclusion that the wise do not always get rewards in life. Such texts remind us again that wisdom was part of the culture throughout the ancient Near East. Habel's perspective, however, is quite broad and takes no account of the specific setting in ancient Israel's tradition.

Jerald Janzen's commentary suggests that we read Job in light of the history of religion. The broader setting has been described as humans moving from seeing the divine in terms of natural power to the model of kings with slaves to the perspective of personal deities. Job could, then, be a response to the tendency to arrogantly manipulate a personal deity. In the history of ancient Israelite religion, the book of Job could mark the move from the older, simple religion to a religion that embraces the ambiguity of life. Janzen suggests that Job changes and deepens the tradition reflected in the Old Testament, and he seeks to interpret the book in light of a variety of other Old Testament texts.

In chapter 2 I mentioned the work of Brevard Childs who emphasizes the canon as the context for interpretation. He suggests that when we read Job in that setting, we see it more specifically as a wisdom book in dialogue with other wisdom texts, especially the book of Proverbs. In that dialogue Job offers a corrective to the wisdom tradition, a corrective that suggests human wisdom does not have all the answers for life. I have already proposed that Job is a wisdom dialogue, and so it is reasonable to read the book in conversation with Proverbs on the nature of wisdom.

## Job and Theology

Before we embark on our journey through the text of Job, it might be helpful to raise the question of what the book is about. What is the central issue in the book? Consider the following possibilities:

- *Suffering*—A better label would be undeserved suffering. The problem is that the book does not address suffering directly except in the Elihu speeches, and the perspective of those speeches does not seem to fit Job's circumstance.

- *Theodicy*—Some commentators describe the book as a defense of God's justice in the face of Job's suffering. This view is rather theoretical for a book that seems so close to real life.

- *Retribution*—The traditional doctrine of reward and retribution came to explain life in a mechanistic way: Do good, and get reward; do evil, and get judgment. The example of Job contradicts that articulation of the moral order of life, but I question whether the basic purpose of the book would be to negate a particular view.

- *Encounter with God*—H. H. Rowley suggests that the book is about encounter with God in the midst of crisis. God comes to Job. This perspective is important in the book but does not tie the book to its Old Testament setting.

- *Disinterested Righteousness*—James Crenshaw suggests that the issue in Job is articulated in Job 1:9: Does Job fear God for nothing? Is Job faithful because of the reward or only for the sake of being righteous? This issue is certainly present, but does it square with the plot of the whole book?

- *Limits of Wisdom*—The epilogue to the book suggests with the restoration of Job that life makes sense. What the book has inserted in that wisdom perspective is ambiguity. There are unexplainables in life. There are limits to human wisdom.

The book of Job is about a web of issues; I have listed six. All are relevant. I have suggested that Job is a wisdom dialogue and that we read it in the context of ancient Israel's wisdom movement. In that canonical sense, the book explores the inner and outer limits of human wisdom. There is a sense to life, and it is a sense that includes the unexplainable—like Job's suffering. God has given some, but not all, wisdom to humans. Perhaps this exploration of the limits of human wisdom is the umbrella under which we can consider the varied issues Job treats. We now continue our journey into the text of Job. You will need to keep the biblical text at hand. The journey will hold twists and turns.

## Content

### Job 1–14

The book's prologue sets up the story of the major character Job. The first chapter begins by introducing Job as the paradigmatic wise man. Job "was blameless and upright, one who feared God and turned away from evil." Up to this point, Job's life had confirmed the traditional doctrine of reward and retribution. He had the full reward of family and possessions. In verse 5, Job's concern anticipates that misfortune could befall his family. With verse 6, the scene changes suddenly to the throne room of God.

The council of the Lord is in session. Other Old Testament texts also speak of this gathering of divine messengers—for instance, 1 Kings 22 and Zechariah 3. These "heavenly beings" we might call angels, but they are angels not in the sense of harps and wings and feathers, but in the sense of messengers, which is what the Hebrew word means. Among the council is the Satan. The Hebrew word is not a personal name but a title, the confuser or adversary or accuser or even prosecuting attorney. God says to the Satan, "Where have you been?" The Accuser replies, "I have been ranging to and fro on the earth testing the faith of humans." God wonders if the Satan has considered Job and repeats the description of Job as the ideal wise person, "a blameless and upright man who fears God and turns away from evil" (v. 8). The Satan replies that of course Job is faithful because he gets such reward of family and possessions for his faith. Thus begins the test of Job's faith. God agrees to the contest of removing the rewards to see if Job remains faithful. God risks trusting Job's integrity.

The scenes in these introductory chapters alternate between earth and heaven and so we return to the earthly setting of Job (1:13-22). Job receives the horrendous word by way of three messengers that his livestock and servants have been taken or destroyed. A fourth messenger brings the deathly news that Job's daughters and sons have been killed. Job responds with all the symbols of grief and with the famous cry articulating the human condition, "Naked I came from my mother's womb, and naked shall I return there; the Lord gave, and the Lord has taken away; blessed be the name of the Lord." The concluding note of the chapter is essential to the story: Job has withstood the test and remained faithful. Chapter 2 begins with a repeat of the scene in the divine throne room. Now the Satan receives permission to test Job's faith even to the point of inflicting a disease upon Job.

In the final earthly scene, Job now suffers the pain of an indescribable disease. Imagine the worst disease and exaggerate that. Job sits on the ash heap and scrapes his sores with a potsherd but maintains his integrity, even in the face of his wife's commentary. She suggests that he curse God and die, but Job says one must take the good and the bad from God. As the heavenly council had gathered earlier, the earthly council gathers at the end of chapter 3 when Eliphaz, Bildad, and Zophar come to visit Job in his misery. The three are shocked at his condition and symbolize their grief. They all sit in silence for seven days. Job's suffering is beyond description. These opening chapters have plotted a severe test of Job's faith and wisdom. The character Job, of course, does not know that it is a test; he only knows that he suffers intensely. Also at stake is traditional wisdom's explanation of the course of life.

With chapter 3, the book moves to poetry and the haunting opening lament of Job. In this powerful cry, Job begins by cursing the day on which he was born. He wishes that the creation of Genesis 1 would be undone and that he had never seen the light of any day. This chapter is one of the darkest in the Old Testament, along with Psalm 88 and Jeremiah 20. Job wishes that he had been stillborn and never come into this life that is now filled with trouble and woe. Death would be better.

> Why is light given to one who cannot see the way,
>     whom God has fenced in? (v. 23)

There are only sighs and groans. The concluding line of the chapter captures Job's plight: "I have no rest; but trouble comes." Job was initially introduced as the example of a prosperous, wise man. Now he is in the depths of trouble and despair.

The poetic dialogue begins in earnest with chapter 4. The first cycle of speeches is in chapters 4–14. Eliphaz, Bildad, and Zophar each make a speech, and Job responds to each. The three have come to "comfort" Job and use this dialogue format. They do not offer much real comfort, but the fact that they sit with Job in mourning for a week before speaking does enable us to be somewhat sympathetic toward them. As you read these chapters, consider the question of what might be the theme of this cycle of speeches.

Eliphaz speaks in chapters 4–5. He begins by establishing the wisdom setting for the speech and relating it to Job's suffering. He works from observation. Job as a sage has instructed others and should now yield to his own wisdom, "your fear of God" (v. 4), as he suffers. Eliphaz has observed life and seen its order. God rewards the upright and brings down the wicked. Eliphaz also claims a revelation in a night vision: humans are but subject to divine whims. The advice Eliphaz gives to Job is to submit to God; therein is his only hope. God is the controller of all destinies, and so Job should come back to God in the hope of redemption. Job's suffering is from a just God and, in line with traditional wisdom, Eliphaz says Job should confess to God. Job responds in chapters 6–7 by describing his anguish and maintaining his innocence (v. 10). Job's companions offer no help. Job responds to Eliphaz that he will attend to honest words.

> Teach me, and I will be silent;
>> make me understand how I have gone wrong.
> How forceful are honest words!
>> But your reproof, what does it reprove? (6:24-25)

Job will be honest and asks the same from the three visitors. He continues to describe his plight as one of a slave in the first verses of chapter 7. He is in desperation and wishes for death.

> I loathe my life; I would not live forever.
> Let me alone, for my days are a breath. (7:16)

In the concluding verses of chapter 7, Job alludes to Psalm 8 but reverses the meaning.

> What are human beings, that you make so much of them,
>> that you set your mind on them,
> visit them every morning,
>> test them every moment? (vv. 17-18)

The attention Job receives from God is harsh, and so Job seeks a reprieve. Job cries, "Why do I suffer so? Why do you not pardon me, O God?" Job seems to be fading away, all too slowly.

Bildad's first speech is in chapter 8. The source of authority for him is the wisdom past generations have handed down. That wisdom trusts the justice of God, and so Job should repent rather than rave against God. He also, in a classic wisdom move, appeals to nature.

> Can papyrus grow where there is no marsh?
> Can reeds flourish where there is no water? (v. 11)

Just so, those who forget God will fade. Job should repent and submit to God. Job responds in the next two chapters. The first verses of chapter 9 take a different tack. Job agrees that God is the one who controls creation, but Job can't seem to get an audience with this God. Job's suffering and anger are described eloquently. At the end of chapter 9, Job pleads for a truce in the divine warfare waged against him so that he might make his case before the Almighty. He boldly uses legal language to request a hearing. Job seems to be moving to deeper issues and already exhibits the tendency to look past the three companions and on to God. Job is experiencing the overpowering effects of chaos. God has created Job and now, seemingly capriciously, watches to oppress him. Job is gripped by the power of death and wishes death would fully come.

Chapter 11 presents the first speech of Zophar. He begins by responding to Job in almost a sarcastic voice. Surely Job would not suggest that he is innocent and God is in the wrong! Does Job know the mind of God? God properly determines fates in life.

> For he knows those who are worthless;
>> when he sees iniquity, will he not consider it?
> But a stupid person will get understanding,
>> when a wild ass is born human. (11:11-12)

Job's proper response is to get right with God and then hope for life will come. Zophar's direct address to Job clarifies the position of the three visitors. Job responds in chapters 12–14. He is persistent, but his ambivalence about God becomes clearer in chapter 12. God is creator and ruler. God has wisdom but seems to use it to bring contempt on people such as Job. In chapter 13, Job continues to press his legal defense and seek an audience before God. He warns his dialogue partners that they will suffer if they speak falsely, even to defend God (v. 7). Their words do not help Job.

> Your maxims are proverbs of ashes,
>> your defenses are defenses of clay. (v. 12)

Job continues to plead boldly for an audience with the real enemy and only hope, the Almighty. Job refers to nature and the tree. If it is cut down, it may bud forth again, but humans have no such hope (14:7-10). Humans are simply at an end. Remember that for most of the Old Testament, there is no life after death. The dead go to Sheol. Belief in a life beyond, a resurrection, emerges at the end of the Old Testament era. Job's description of the human condition in chapter 14 is dismal, and for Job, God is both revealed and hidden. In this first cycle of speeches, the nature of God is one of the major themes. For Eliphaz, Bildad, and Zophar, God rewards the upright and punishes the sinful. Job is in the middle of horrific pain.

## Job 15–31

The second cycle of speeches is in chapters 15–21. Again, it might help focus our attention to consider whether this cycle has a general theme. The second speech by Eliphaz begins the cycle in chapter 15. Another way to approach these texts would be to consider whether the speeches of each character have a theme. Eliphaz certainly affirms traditional wisdom as he did in chapters 4–5. He accuses Job, in the first verses of chapter 15, of seeking to destroy wisdom. He suggests that Job's own words work against Job. Eliphaz affirms the authority of traditional wisdom and emphasizes Job's alleged wickedness. God certainly cannot trust Job. The last part of the speech vividly describes the unfortunate fate of the wicked. This speech is an example of how the characters in this drama do not know what went on in the prologue. Eliphaz also seems to miss how overwhelming is the disaster Job faces. Job responds in the next two chapters. Is there an umbrella theme in Job's speeches?

Then Job answered:
>  "I have heard many such things;
>  miserable comforters are you all." (16:1-2)

It is clear now that Job understands his troubles to be of divine origin (v. 9), and yet he maintains his innocence (v. 17). Job sees his life and dreams at an end and sees little hope. He continues to face public disdain. Will he and his hope both go to Sheol, to death?

The second speech of Bildad is in chapter 18. He directs a frontal assault upon Job and affirms the fate of the wicked.

>  Surely the light of the wicked is put out,
>    and the flame of their fire does not shine. (v. 5)

The implication is that Job is among those. Job replies in a famous text, chapter 19. Job begins to feel isolated. Neither the visitors nor God is really hearing his plea. Even Job's closest friends and family have rejected him as he fades away. In the last verses of the chapter, Job eloquently pleads his case and breaks through to a word of hope.

>  For I know that my Redeemer lives,
>    and that at the last he will stand upon the earth. (v. 25)

The Redeemer, or *go'el,* was usually the next of kin and had several functions in ancient Israel. That person would buy back land that had been lost, or redeem the next of kin from slavery, or take on a deceased brother's wife in the custom of levirate marriage, or avenge death. Who is the Redeemer here? The function seems to be securing an audience with God. It is often suggested that this audience will be in an afterlife. This text may be one of those near the time of the Babylonian exile and after, a text that catches a glimpse of an afterlife. Here the perspective would be that Job has faced intense suffering; perhaps he could encounter God beyond the trouble of this life. Readers will be able to tell, however, from the notes in English translations of Job 19:23-29 that this text witnesses a number of difficulties in translation as well as interpretation. The text is problematic. At the same time, it does appear to offer a word of hope, a welcome relief in this dialogue.

Zophar's speech is in chapter 20. He emphasizes the justly deserved fate of the wicked. They will come to naught. They reap the consequences of their evil lifestyle.

> In full sufficiency they will be in distress;
>> all the force of misery will come upon them. (v. 22)

God brings the wicked to destruction. The fate of the wicked does seem to be the theme of this cycle of speeches. Job responds in chapter 21. He maintains his innocence but rejects the argument that the wicked get what they deserve. He rather argues that the wicked prosper, again working from the observation of a sage. The dialogue between these sages appears to get rather heated.

> How then will you comfort me with empty nothings?
>> There is nothing left of your answers but falsehood. (v. 34)

Chapter 22 sees the beginning of the third cycle of speeches. Eliphaz begins again. His attack upon Job is a direct one.

> Is not your wickedness great?
>> There is no end to your iniquities. (v. 5)

Job should get right with God. The theme seems to be that Job is sinful. Job's reply is in chapters 23–24. Job again boldly seeks an audience with God and uses the legal language of putting his case before God, but God is not to be found.

> If I go forward, he is not there;
>> or backward, I cannot perceive him;
> on the left he hides, and I cannot behold him;
>> I turn to the right, but I cannot see him. (23:8-9)

As with the speakers of the lament psalms, Job searches for God; he seeks the divine presence. In chapter 24, Job vividly describes the wicked and complains that they prosper. The latter part of the chapter is somewhat confusing for it seems also to say that the wicked will suffer full consequences for their sin. Is Job quoting some other source, or is another character speaking? The concluding part of this chapter anticipates the textual difficulties in the remainder of the dialogue. Could those problems be reflective of the problems in the dialogue?

Bildad's speech is in chapter 25. He denigrates the place of humans in creation and suggests that people cannot be righteous before God. Other creation texts in the Old Testament such as Psalm 8 or Genesis 1 emphasize God's relationship with persons as God's creations. Bildad exaggerates the distance from the creator. Humans are of little worth in his view. The remaining chapters of this third cycle of speeches are problematic. It is difficult to know who is speaking. H. H. Rowley has constructed the following possibility:

- Bildad speaks in 25 and 26:5-14.
- Job replies in 26:1-4 and 27:1-6.
- Zophar's speech, which does not appear in the text as we have it, Rowley identifies as 27:7-12, 24:18-24, and 27:13-23.
- Job completes the cycle of speeches in 29–31.

This approach has been typical of commentators; the text is confusing.

A different approach is simply to admit that there are problems of interpretation at this point. Perhaps the breakdown in the text is reflective of a breakdown in the dialogue. It has not been fruitful. It is coming unraveled and fading away in confusion. The text has Job speaking in chapter 26. Apparently, he begins by heaping sarcastic praise upon the three visitors; he goes on to say that God is mighty but not understood. Job is confused. In the opening verses of chapter 27, Job speaks of his integrity. It is all he has left. He will not relinquish his honesty. He continues to maintain that he does not deserve the suffering he has endured. Integrity has to do with wholeness of life, a life in line with the perspective one espouses. Some have suggested that 27:7-23 should be attributed to Zophar, but others support the attribution to Job. These verses see the fall of the wicked.

Job 28 is a hymn to wisdom. It speaks of the search for wisdom.

> Where then does wisdom come from?
>     And where is the place of understanding?
> It is hidden from the eyes of all living,
>     and concealed from the birds of the air. (vv. 20-21).

God is the one who knows where wisdom is to be found and
how to get there. God has given wisdom to humans, but not all
wisdom.

> And he said to humankind,
>> "Truly, the fear of the Lord, that is wisdom;
>> and to depart from evil is understanding." (v. 28)

The sages and their students can learn much, but not all.

Job makes a final plea in chapters 29–31. In powerful and
poignant language, he contrasts his earlier prosperity with his
current ordeal. He has experienced terror and darkness. Light
and the way forward are hidden from him.

> But when I looked for good, evil came;
>> and when I waited for light, darkness came.
> My inward parts are in turmoil, and are never still;
>> days of affliction come to meet me. (30:26-27)

In chapter 31, Job speaks an oath of self-imprecation. If he has
not lived an upright life, may he suffer great punishment. Job
espouses a high standard of ethics and affirms such as characteristic of his life. The chapter serves as a strong protestation of
innocence and a final plea for deliverance. Job calls upon God to
hear and answer this faithful servant. This conclusion of the
third cycle of speeches anticipates that the book's conflict is
moving toward a climax.

## Job 32–42

With the conclusion of Job's words at the end of chapter 31, we
take a breath on this roller coaster ride that is our journey
through Job. The beginning of chapter 32 notes that Job now
feels self-justified, and that while the three companions believe
Job to be wrong, the dialogue has come to naught. Then suddenly the character Elihu bursts on the scene. He is a kind of
"angry young man" who seeks to correct the failure of the three
visitors and straighten out Job. Many scholars see the Elihu
speeches as an addition to the book, but these chapters still serve
important functions. They emphasize many of the arguments of
the friends and seek to correct Job. Some of Elihu's statements
are sufficiently exaggerated to make it possible to read them as

irony. Elihu views Job's suffering as disciplinary, which does not square with the prologue. Finally, the last part of the Elihu speeches help the transition to the divine speeches in theme and style. So Elihu defends God's justice and majesty, in the face of Job, and asserts that Job's suffering is disciplinary.

Elihu makes four speeches; there are no responses. The first speech is in chapters 32–33. Here Elihu says Job's claim of injustice is false; God answers prayer. Elihu comes on the scene, having waited impatiently for the older speakers to finish. He claims that his youth will be wiser than the age of the three visitors. Indeed, it is the failure of the visitors that moved Elihu to intervene. He now summons Job. Elihu says that Job's claim of innocence and unjust treatment is false and defends God. Job's claim that God does not answer is contradicted by experience.

> For God speaks in one way,
>     and in two, though people do not perceive it. (33:14)

Elihu pleads for Job to listen to his wisdom (v. 33).

The second speech is in chapter 34. Here Elihu defends the character of God against Job, who is now characterized as impious. Job's claim that God is unjust is false. God is instead impartial and knows all. Elihu understands that he is exposing Job as foolish and rebellious against God.

The third speech, chapter 35, claims that righteousness and sin affect people, contrary to Job's claim. Wickedness and righteousness do not affect God, but they do affect people. When people act in upright or evil ways, it has an impact on other people. On the other hand, God is already perfect, and so human actions do not add or detract from God. When the cry of the oppressed is not heard, it is because they do not cry aright.

> Surely God does not hear an empty cry,
>     nor does the Almighty regard it. (v. 13)

> Job opens his mouth in empty talk,
>     he multiplies words without knowledge. (v. 16)

Elihu's final speech comes to the point that affliction has a purpose in the view of the majestic God. Chapter 36 argues that suffering is disciplinary and that Job's suffering fits that view.

> He delivers the afflicted by their affliction,
>     and opens their ear by adversity. (v. 15)

The conclusion of Elihu's words anticipates the divine speeches to follow.

> God thunders wondrously with his voice;
>     he does great things that we cannot comprehend. (37:5)

God's work in nature is majestic and unfathomable.

With chapter 38, we come to the divine speeches out of the whirlwind. God comes to Job in a theophany, a divine appearance, and makes two powerful, eloquent speeches. The theme is that God, not Job, rules the mysteries of creation. The first speech, chapters 38–39, affirms that the mysteries of creation are beyond Job. God, the giver of light, addresses Job and makes clear that the mysteries of earth and sky are beyond Job's understanding.

> Where were you when I laid the foundation of the earth?
>     Tell me, if you have understanding.
> Who determined its measurements—surely you know!
>     Or who stretched the line upon it? (38:4-5)

> Or who shut in the sea with doors
>     when it burst out from the womb? (v. 8)

The mysteries of animal and bird life are also beyond Job's understanding. Can Job make animals give birth or control the mysteries of birds? Job responds to this first speech with silence.

The second divine speech begins with verse 6 of chapter 40 and continues through chapter 41. The theme continues with the affirmation that the rule of the universe is beyond Job. God questions Job: Can you rule the universe? Do you understand Behemoth and Leviathan? These great creatures of the deep, often identified as the hippopotamus and crocodile, are only under the rule of the creator, not under the rule of Job.

> On earth it [Leviathan] has no equal,
>     a creature without fear.
> It surveys everything that is lofty;
>     it is king over all that are proud. (41:33-34)

Yahweh's questioning of Job makes it clear that Job is but human and not lord of creation. The divine response to Job is intriguing because God does not speak to Job's suffering or questions. But God does appear and by way of this encounter with the divine, Job's darkness and indifference leave. Job begins to see the place of humans in the creation. His conflict is moving to resolution.

Job's final response is in 42:1-6 and has to do with wisdom. He has changed in perspective and now sees that he does not know all. His view of things is different after the encounter with Yahweh. Job kept his integrity but now sees that life includes what is unexplainable. The encounter with God has made it possible for Job to move forward.

> I had heard of you by the hearing of the ear,
>> but now my eye sees you;
> therefore I despise myself,
>> and repent in dust and ashes. (vv. 5-6)

The translation of verse 6 is quite difficult. The New Jewish Version gives a helpful alternative rendering.

> I recant and relent, being but dust and ashes.

Job does not suggest that he deserved his suffering, but he accepts his humanity and changes his perspective. There are limits to what he knows.

The prose epilogue completes the book. It begins with a divine rebuke of Eliphaz, Bildad, and Zophar. The clear verdict is that they were in the wrong and Job was in the right. Job was the one who pursued matters with a genuine and honest faith. The three are to make atoning sacrifice and, with a touch of irony, God's servant Job is to intercede for them. The scene is cast in wisdom terminology. In the wisdom dialogue, Job has spoken aright. The setting reminds readers of the prologue. The book's frame is completed.

In the concluding paragraph, God acts to restore Job. Job's possessions are doubled, and he is surrounded with family and friends. The numbers given indicate how wealthy Job now is. Job also receives seven sons and three daughters. The daughters are praised and given inheritance along with their brothers, an unusual act of equality for the world of ancient Israel. The book concludes with Job dying as an old man, blessed and wise. Job has lived a full life. The restoration of Job suggests that there is an order to life, but the book makes it clear that life also includes ambiguity. The positive conclusion does not negate Job's trauma; the unexplainable is still part of life that God has created.

## Conclusion

Our journey with Job has been an intense one of many twists and turns. The book speaks to a complex web of issues. I have suggested a number of them: undeserved suffering, theodicy, God's presence in the midst of crisis, disinterested righteousness, views of retribution, the limits of wisdom. The book continues to attract attention because readers identify with the struggle. Job struggles mightily. His questioning is affirmed, but his questions are not answered. What is met is the cry for a genuine encounter with the divine. That encounter explores the inner and outer limits of human wisdom, and perhaps that is the most central issue in the book. There is a sense to life, but it includes the unexplainable. Such a perspective fits our journey into the wisdom tradition of the Old Testament. It also makes the book particularly profound today, a day in which many religionists through various media claim to have the answers of life. Job says, "Beware! The fear of the Lord, that is wisdom."

## For Further Reading

Balentine, Samuel E. "Job, Book of." In *Mercer Dictionary of the Bible*, ed. Watson Mills, 455-56. Macon GA: Mercer University Press, 1990.

Childs, Brevard. *Introduction to the Old Testament as Scripture*, 526-44. Philadelphia: Fortress Press, 1979.

Crenshaw, James L. "Job, Book of." In *Anchor Bible Dictionary*, Vol. 3, 858-68. New York: Doubleday, 1992.

_____. *Old Testament Wisdom: An Introduction*. Atlanta: John Knox Press, 1981.

Habel, Norman C. *The Book of Job: A Commentary*. Old Testament Library. Philadelphia: Westminster Press, 1985.

Janzen, J. Gerald. *Job*. Interpretation, A Bible Commentary for Teaching and Preaching. Atlanta: John Knox Press, 1985.

Murphy, Roland E. *The Tree of Life: An Exploration of Biblical Wisdom Literature.* The Anchor Bible Reference Library. New York: Doubleday, 1990.

Rowley, H. H. *Job.* New Century Bible. Grand Rapids: Wm. B. Eerdmans Publishing Co., 1976.

Westermann, Claus. *The Structure of the Book of Job: A Form-Critical Analysis.* Philadelphia: Fortress Press, 1981.

# Chapter 7

# Ecclesiastes
# Search for Meaning

Our final wisdom book is the book of Ecclesiastes. Like Job, it is a book of speculative wisdom, asking many questions about life and its meaning. The form and approach of the book are rather different. The book is not as well known as Job, in part because its interpretation is riddled with a number of ambiguities. In this chapter we will consider some background issues and then look at the text as a way of enabling readers to enter Ecclesiastes and struggle with its significance.

## Background

### Title

The Hebrew title of the book is *Qoheleth*. Since Martin Luther, the tradition has been to translate the term "Preacher," but it is probably more accurate to translate it "Teacher." The form in Hebrew is a feminine participle, a form that can be used for those who hold offices. The term is probably a title rather than a personal name. The Hebrew root word relates to the gathered congregation or assembly. So the title most likely indicates that this book is the wisdom of the Teacher of the gathered community of faith. The English title comes from the Greek (Septuagint) and Latin (Vulgate) versions of the Old Testament and is associated with the Greek word for church, again the gathered community.

## Authorship

Solomon is traditionally listed as the author of Ecclesiastes. The opening heading of the book suggests such: "The words of the Teacher, the son of David, King in Jerusalem." The description of Qoheleth in the remainder of chapter 1, especially verses 12 and 16, and in chapter 2 is intended to bring King Solomon to mind. At the same time, the name "Solomon" is never used in the book, and the latter part of the book speaks about the king rather than appearing to be the words of the king. Could the reference to Solomon mean something other than authorship?

Brevard Childs offers a helpful way forward when he suggests that the allusion to Solomon is a way to say that the wisdom in this book is in the tradition of the great patron saint of wisdom in Israel, even King Solomon. Our journey into the book will suggest that at times Ecclesiastes says things that were not part of the mainstream in ancient Israel. It is thus important to affirm that this book is true wisdom in the line of the great wise teacher Solomon. In any case, the author is one who has experienced much of life and looks back on it. Qoheleth has enjoyed wealth and pleasure and travel and reflects on a broad experience of life and the world.

## Setting

We have seen that the search for wisdom is reflected in the literature of the whole ancient Near East and that broader context is important for the task of interpretation. Many scholars would suggest that at points Ecclesiastes reflects concerns present in the Hellenistic or Greek world. The book is certainly part of the wisdom tradition in the Old Testament and needs to be read as such; it is in dialogue with the popular royal wisdom reflected in Proverbs. Most would suggest that the book is in the form of a royal testament. One of the NRSV headings is "Reflections of a Royal Philosopher." Qoheleth looks back on life and passes on a legacy of wisdom for the next generation. The writer includes a number of proverbs in this testament of wisdom.

## Date

One's decision on the question of authorship obviously affects one's view of the date of Ecclesiastes. Most scholars suggest that the book is one of the later documents in the Old Testament. Third century B.C.E. is a reasonable date. The book's language appears to be some of the latest in the Old Testament. The book and its perspective seem to fit best that environment.

## Structure

Questions about the structure and composition of Ecclesiastes remain difficult to answer. Most interpreters would agree that the book begins with an introductory poem, found in 1:2-11, and that a concluding poem begins with 11:7 and continues through 12:8. An epilogue concludes the book. In addition, we might divide the book into two main sections. The refrain of the first part, 1:12–6:9, is, "This is vanity and a chasing after wind." The refrain of the second section is a variation of "knowing/not knowing" and "finding out/not finding out." The refrains suggest the subject matter. Our journey into the book will tentatively follow this structure.

J. A. Loader suggests that the book moves on sets of polarities and the tensions between them. The book presents one thought and then a counterthought. Vanity in life and the reality of God are in tension as are involvement in life and withdrawal from life. The book uses typical wisdom sayings and criticizes them. Readers will notice tensions in the book. The structure of the book is something of an enigma with its many questions and repetitions, which is probably intentional since the book seems to view life as an enigma. Qoheleth begins with the question of what makes sense of life and conducts a series of tests to answer the question. Is it pleasure, wisdom, wealth, or something else? The sage does not find an answer, but the epilogue then places the reflection in the context of the Old Testament wisdom tradition. Life is a question, and the best way forward is reverence for God and the commandments.

## Ecclesiastes and Theology

Most interpreters describe Ecclesiastes as a book of *skepticism*. It is more than doubt and questioning; it is an affirmation of uncertainty. The book presents a pessimistic view of life. James Crenshaw's treatment represents this view. He labels the book as "The Chasing after Meaning" and suggests that Qoheleth affirms a number of theses: Death cancels everything; wisdom cannot achieve its goal; God is unknowable; the world is crooked; pleasure commends itself.

This pessimistic view of the book does not, in my judgment, sufficiently consider its wisdom context. By the time Qoheleth comes on the scene, the wisdom explanation of life seems to have fossilized into a mechanistic doctrine that suggests good causes reward, and evil causes punishment. God is in a cause-and-effect straightjacket, and the mystery of life has been explained. The sayings, questions, and tensions in Ecclesiastes react to such a perspective. The primary affirmation of the book thus seems to be the *freedom of God*. God, not humans, gives life. Under this affirmation of the freedom of God, Qoheleth commends three courses of action for humans.

- Do not attempt to be perfect (7:16-17).
- Make the most of life (5:18-20).
- Help each other (4:9-12).

A parable might illustrate the message. A farmer lives on an island on a poor plot of land. He knows that he will not leave the island, but his neighbors keep saying there is a new world beyond the surrounding waters, a new world that will solve all problems. The farmer can complain about the plight life has brought, or he can be about making the poor plot of land the best possible. Ecclesiastes affirms that humans do not control what comes in life. Only God is free to determine that. Humans can be about making the most of the life given.

Ecclesiastes causes readers to stop and think. It is an honest and haunting book that asks questions and will not accept conventional answers. The conclusion of the book puts the questions in the context of faith. I do not interpret the book to be so pessimistic. Some have proposed that it is a bleak picture of life without Christ. This view does not consider the book's

Old Testament context. Ecclesiastes as a wisdom book affirms that the shape of life is beyond human control; only God is free to give life. The human community is to make the most of life in this context. The book deepens the wisdom tradition and explores the boundaries of faith. It is important that the Old Testament canon includes such questions for contemporary readers. Qoheleth's world held many intriguing and troubling questions; so does ours. Chaos is knocking at the door. Qoheleth's reflections on life are an important part of wisdom's guide for life and faith.

## Contents

### Ecclesiastes 1

After the heading, the book begins with its theme statement.

> Vanity of vanities, says the Teacher,
> vanity of vanities! All is vanity. (v. 2)

"Vanity of vanities" is a way in Hebrew to say "the most vain thing." The term "vanity" includes what is ephemeral and futile. What people experience is brief and fruitless. The remainder of the introductory poem illustrates the point. The cycles of the generations, the sun, the wind, and rivers all show that there is nothing new. The sage observes the sameness of life. New things do not come; only those same continuous cycles come again and again. It is helpful to read this poem in its wisdom context. It is not a comment about the emptiness of all of life. It is a comment about the brevity and futility of a wisdom that has explained everything in life. God and life are more mysterious.

This perspective continues in the rest of the opening chapter. Qoheleth is looking back on life and reflecting. Life seems so difficult to grasp. Even wisdom does not provide the answer. Life is "crooked" in the sense that it cannot be trusted to bring forth the predicted results. Again, the perspective questions a wisdom that leaves no room for mystery. These concluding verses of chapter 1 (vv. 12-18) anticipate what is to follow. The sage reflects on life and searches for its significance. Qoheleth is passing on wisdom by reporting a testing of life. The following series of experiments searches for the sense to life. The search is one of intrigue and of struggle.

## Ecclesiastes 2:1–6:9

Ecclesiastes 2:1–6:9 pursues the experiments to find what gives life meaning. The first try is pleasure, and the beginning of chapter 2 describes the various pleasures of the great sage, but pleasure is judged to be "vanity and a chasing after wind" (v. 11). Qoheleth tries pleasure, wisdom, and success but finds none of the three to bring meaning to life. Chapter 2 comments often on wisdom and folly. Wisdom is clearly better but does not bring the full meaning that traditional wisdom teachers claimed. The chapter concludes with the theme of this part of the book: "This also is vanity and a chasing after wind."

Chapter 3 begins with the famous poem on the times of life. It also trades in polarities put in the parallel structure of Hebrew poetry. The issue is deciding which time it is in life and seizing the moment. The difficulty is that for humans, discovering the proper time is an ongoing puzzle. There is then a rhythm to life, a rhythm given by God but hardly available to humans.

Chapter 4 continues with the theme of polarities in human existence. It is better to avoid the extremes of life and attempt to see the way through life's ambiguity. In this process, relationships are helpful, but only relatively so, as with everything else. The concluding verses of chapter 4 may reflect the specific setting of the book. Perhaps the sage is teaching a class of prominent, wealthy youth in Jerusalem.

Chapter 5 continues the warning against excesses in life and yet, people are still to make the most of the life they are given. Verses 18-20 is a kind of summary of the latter advice, under the freedom of God.

> This is what I have seen to be good: it is fitting to eat and drink and find enjoyment in all the toil with which one toils under the sun the few days of the life God gives us; for this is our lot. Likewise all to whom God gives wealth and possessions and whom he enables to enjoy them, and to accept their lot and find enjoyment in their toil—this is the gift of God. For they will scarcely brood over the days of their lives, because God keeps them occupied with the joy of their hearts.

Ecclesiastes 6:1-9 sums up the first major part of the book. The polarities of human existence are important to Qoheleth. The sage has considered blessing and vanity and concludes that possessions are not the key to life. Labor and insatiability also come under scrutiny; income is not what brings sense to life. Wisdom and folly as well as possessions and death are considered. Life is full of trouble, and Qoheleth's conclusion is the now familiar refrain, "This also is vanity and a chasing after wind." Life remains an enigma, a puzzle.

## Ecclesiastes 6:10–11:6

Ecclesiastes 6:10–11:6 concentrates on knowing and finding out, or perhaps more properly not knowing the future or what is good to do in life. The concluding verse of the first section of chapter 7 summarizes the point well.

> In the day of prosperity be joyful, and in the day of adversity consider; God has made the one as well as the other, so that mortals may not find out anything that will come after them. (v. 14)

Qoheleth considers all of life: good and evil, life and death, wisdom and folly, silence and speech, the pressures of life, prosperity, and God. One is better off with wisdom than without it but only relatively so; it is best not to err to the extremes of life (vv. 15-17). Qoheleth continues to search fervently for meaning. The book suggests that Qoheleth's perspective is more honest, but it does not settle the meaning of life. The sage would support the view that the unexamined life is not worth living, but the examined life is still an enigma.

The theme continues in chapter 8. Humans do not know God or wisdom, what is right or wrong, or what the future holds. Such is true for the righteous and the wicked, the powerless and those with political power. So the sage's advice is to accept life as it is given. Verse 15 is another summary statement of Qoheleth's wisdom.

> So I commend enjoyment, for there is nothing better for people under the sun than to eat, and drink, and enjoy themselves, for this will go with them in their toil through the days of life that God gives them under the sun.

A similar perspective is summarized in 9:7-10. Time and chance come to all. Qoheleth continues to challenge orthodox wisdom. Wisdom is a worthy goal but will not remove the uncertainty of life. People should thus take care in their speaking and other actions.

> Wisdom is better than weapons of war,
>     but one bungler destroys much good. (9:18)

The course of life is not known to humans, and so one is wise to be diligent in covering the possibilities (11:5-6).

### Ecclesiastes 11:7–12:14

Ecclesiastes 11:7–12:8 constitutes a closing poem on youth and old age, a poem that confirms Qoheleth's teaching. The young should enjoy the pleasures of life as they come, for old age will bring diminished joy. The poet aptly describes the difficulties of aging; "grinding" is apparently a reference to the difficulty of chewing in old age. The poem concludes with the book's theme, the theme with which the book began. The reference once again is to what is ephemeral and futile.

> Vanity of vanities, says the Teacher; all is vanity. (12:8)

The book's concluding verses constitute an epilogue, an editorial comment on the book. It commends Qoheleth's wisdom and warns against heeding advice beyond that of the sages. The conclusion of verse 12 is often echoed by students: "Of making many books there is no end, and much study is a weariness of the flesh." The final verses put the book in the context of faith. One is to revere God and keep the commandments; that is the wiser way forward in the face of Qoheleth's perspective on life. God is still the one who is free to give life. The book teaches how to live in that context.

## Conclusion

Ecclesiastes is a book of realism and honesty and of teaching how to deal with life in the face of such a realistic perspective. It is important that Qoheleth's questions and cautions are part of the biblical text. The book affirms that only God is free to give and shape life. So humans are to accept life and make the most of it in community and be careful to avoid the extremes of human existence. The book commends wisdom, but it also is only of relative value; ambiguity is well imprinted in the human experience. Qoheleth's wisdom is a valuable caution and balance whenever we forget and think we can control life and the future, as individuals and as communities.

## For Further Reading

Childs, Brevard. *Introduction to the Old Testament as Scripture,* 580-89. Philadelphia: Fortress Press, 1979.

Crenshaw, James L. "Ecclesiastes, Book of." In *Anchor Bible Dictionary.* Vol. 2, 271-80. New York: Doubleday, 1992.

Crenshaw, James L. *Old Testament Wisdom: An Introduction.* Atlanta: John Knox Press, 1981.

Loader, J. A. *Polar Structures in the Book of Qohelet.* Beihefte zur Zeitschrift für die alttestamentliche Wissenschaft. Berlin: Walter de Gruyter, 1979.

Conclusion

# The Testimony of Poets and Sages

The wisdom tradition continues beyond the Protestant Old Testament. Two apocryphal books are of particular relevance. The first is The Wisdom of Jesus, Son of Sira or Sirach; sometimes the form Ben (son of) Sira is used. Another title derives from the Latin, *Ecclesiasticus.* The book is an anthology of wisdom that is mostly traditional in perspective, though it does reflect a setting in Greek culture. It is usually dated around 180 B.C.E. Here Wisdom is identified with Torah and tied closely to Israel's historical faith traditions. The second document is the Wisdom of Solomon from the first century B.C.E. Greek culture is even more dominant in it, and the book reflects Judaism's struggle with the Hellenistic world. I mention these books to say that wisdom is a living tradition. It continues beyond what Protestants describe as the Old Testament.

## Sages

As our journey into the Old Testament wisdom tradition moves to a close, it is appropriate to summarize the perspectives of the wisdom books. Proverbs provides orthodox observations for successful living and is thus the traditional starting point. It affirms the moral order built into creation. In living the righteous lifestyle, one finds reward. In living the foolish lifestyle, one finds destruction. Walter Brueggemann summarizes the teachings of wisdom in five statements.

- Healthy community life is the goal and meaning of existence.
- Authority for life is discerned in experience.
- Humanity has the primary responsibility for its own destiny and the destiny of its community.
- Life has been called good, that is, life is for human enjoyment, celebration, and appreciation.
- Humanity is celebrated as ruler of the creation.

Popular royal wisdom trusts the world and life and believes a full life is possible for the community. It depends on a creation theology, such as that in Genesis 1, and affirms human responsibility in that creation, which is a gift from God. The sciences and humanities, culture, sex, money, government, play, and table manners are all good gifts from God. Wisdom celebrates the human place in creation, and so some scholars have justifiably called it a biblical humanism.

Proverbs is the orthodox expression of this popular royal wisdom, and I have read Job and Ecclesiastes in dialogue with it. Proverbs provides the base. Job then explores a web of issues: undeserved suffering, theodicy, views of retribution, the divine presence in crises, disinterested righteousness. The primary theme is the limits of human wisdom. There is moral order, but there is also important ambiguity in life. The way forward is not simple but includes questions and struggles and the realization that we will never find all the answers.

Christians may be familiar with the label "the patience of Job" from the New Testament reference James 5:11 where Job is commended as an example. But the word should not be translated "patience." "Endurance/steadfastness" would be more accurate and certainly true to Job's consuming struggle. Job struggles with the chaos in life. Ecclesiastes pushes the dialogue further as the Teacher searches intensely for the meaning of life. God is the one who gives life; the shape of life is beyond human control and so remains a mystery. In that context, people are to make the most of the life they are given, help each other, and avoid extremism. The Teacher presses the boundaries of faith in a brutally realistic reflection on the course of life.

It is important that the Old Testament canon includes the orthodox affirmations of Proverbs and the questions of Job and Ecclesiastes. Both sides of life are important and relevant. The wisdom tradition then moves into the Greek world. Wisdom is keen to see life and to see it in the context of faith. Its books are centered on full living and call people to that gift and task. The chart "A Framework for Reading the Wisdom Books" is a helpful tool for reading Proverbs, Job, and Ecclesiastes as the primary wisdom books.

## Psalmists

The psalmists also included sages, but most of these poets began from the singing of worship. Their songs bear witness to a vibrant faith pilgrimage of dialogue with God. This rich prayer tradition of praise and lament is central to the community's journey through life. The songs articulate faith and keep the people on the journey. As the psalms express faith, they also enable pilgrims to embrace the faith tradition. Sometimes the embracing means full-throated praise; sometimes it means searching questions and challenges. The remarkable prayer poetry of the Psalter touches every facet of life from the poles of plea to praise. The Psalms offer a rich and powerful faith resource.

*****

So our journey of reading comes to an end. Your journey into the books of Psalms, Proverbs, Job, and Ecclesiastes can, however, continue and deepen. My hope is that the words of this volume will help you along the way. With the Psalms, we sing; with Proverbs, Job, and Ecclesiastes, we reflect. Both are essential activities for the community of faith. Good reading and good traveling!

## For Further Reading

Brueggemann, Walter, "Scripture and an Ecumenical Lifestyle: A Study in Wisdom Theology." *Interpretation* 24 (1970): 3-19.
Holladay, William L. *The Psalms through Three Thousand Years: Prayerbook of a Cloud of Witnesses* . Minneapolis: Fortress Press, 1993.

ALL THE BIBLE

ALL THE BIBLE SERIES DESCRIPTION

| AREA | TITLE* |
|---|---|
| Genesis–Deuteronomy | *Journey to the Land of Promise* |
| Former Prophets | *Israel's Rise and Decline* |
| Latter Prophets, excluding Postexilic | *God's Servants, the Prophets* |
| Poetry, Wisdom Literature | *The Testimony of Poets and Sages* |
| Exilic, Postexilic Books | *The Exile and Beyond* |
| The Four Gospels | *The Church's Portraits of Jesus* |
| Acts of the Apostles, Epistles of Paul | *The Church's Mission to the Gentiles* |
| Hebrews–Revelation | *The Church as a Pilgrim People* |

*subject to change